The Judy Collins songbook

The Judy Collins songbook

With comments, instructions and personal reminiscences by

JUDY COLLINS

Music arranged and edited by HERBERT HAUFRECHT

GROSSET & DUNLAP
A NATIONAL GENERAL COMPANY

Publishers / New York

Music Sales Corporation
New York, New York
Exclusive distributors to the music trade

Library of Congress catalog card no. 77-86683
ISBN: 0-448-01918-3

First printing October, 1969
Second printing December, 1969
Third printing February, 1970
Fourth printing March, 1970
Fifth printing August, 1970
Sixth printing November, 1970
Seventh printing November, 1971
Eighth printing March, 1972

Printed in the United States of America.

Dedicated to my mother, Marjorie Byrd Collins

My special thanks to Yafa Lerner, Joseph Greene, and Claudia Lichtblau.

contents

Part 1

In the darkness he would read to us,
His fingers thwarting blindness
With the sound of flesh on paper
Brushing underneath the fantasy
Like the sound of wind moving through the house:
He soothed our fear of the night
With sighing hands.

My father was four when he went blind from glaucoma. When he was five his father, who was a farmer, died. His mother remarried and left the farm to run a gas station in Lapway, Idaho, on the reservation of the Nez Percé Indians. Little Charlie Collins was sent away to the special school in Boise where they sent broken and deformed children to teach them how to live with their unfulfilled dreams, and there his wanderer's life began.

Dad always walked straight, with his shoulders thrown back so that tailors had to remove the bit of material most men need to cover the slight slump of disappointment they wear. In his quiet, brooding nights, he would prowl the backyard in the summer. He had insomnia all his life, because night and day were the same color to him. I remember his nighttime walks in the kitchen, the refrigerator door opening in the dark, peanut butter sandwiches and milk invisibly disappearing into his invisible mouth; mother would say, "Come to bed, Charles, stop roaming around the house." He mowed the lawn most of the time; he went barefoot to feel where he had cut the last row. He had a fetish for polishing shoes with his fingers, rubbing the thick, lush wax into the leather with a kind of craftsman's glee, and then polishing the finish, rubbing till the leather shone under his hands. He laughed a lot and he yelled a lot and used a hairbrush when he spanked me, till I was too old to punish. The only time I remember taking advantage of his blindness was when I was about 11; he and I were having an argument and I stuck my tongue out at him. But mother was walking into the room at the moment and caught me and she spanked me.

Sometimes Mom would drive Dad places, but most of the time he got around the cities on his own, taking the buses and walking. He never used a dog, or a cane, except once when he had a job with the State Rehabilitation Center in Denver, and they insisted that he use a cane. So he got a collapsible one and when anybody official was around he would use it. But he refused to depend on a cane or a dog or even an arm if he could help it. The touch of an elbow was enough, and told him where you were; and the simple system of radar he discovered could guide him through the world of night he woke up to as a child. Vibrations from buildings, rooms, walls, any surface, told him where he was. He could walk into someone's house and in ten minutes he would know it as if it were his own.

He liked to do everything himself except cut up his steak. He would go out to the garage and warm up the car in the morning for mother. Once he ran it through the front of the garage wall. In Seattle, walking down the street, he fell straight into an open man-hole. He came home with a huge blister under his arm and my mother wanted to sue the city for leaving it uncovered, but he wouldn't let her. Mom met him one day in Seattle in 1937 when she offered to help him across the street corner. He yelled at her that he didn't want any help. So she followed him, and it turned out they were taking the same bus. He apologized for being so rude, offered to buy her a soda, and four months later they got married.

Sometimes he stumbled right into tricycles and wagons and skates left in the middle of the sidewalk by his own and other people's children. He would go straight into one of them, and curse and bleed, and fume like W.C. Fields that "anyone who hates children can't be all bad." Daddy read constantly, submerging himself in visions, adventures, maybe remembering dimly the colors from years before. He could read in the dark with the covers pulled up over his head if he wanted to. One time he got the back issues of the *Reader's Digest,* about ten years of magazines, and had to build shelves all across the back of the double garage in our house on Willow Street in Denver. One copy of "The Brothers Karamazov" in Braille took up a whole corner of the room, the huge Braille books spilling all over the house and collecting in great disorderly piles as high as your waist. He taught my three brothers and me and then, finally, my sister, about books and endless trips you can take in them.

> "... every day the man who had no vision
> Read verses streaked and blurred with color.
> Deserts full of calico and rainbow-costumed heroes
> Quilted all his dark days."

My father was an angry man. He was haunted by fear and tied in deep knots of loneliness that were hard for anyone to reach into except maybe his best friend, Holden. They were at the University of Idaho together, and did wild things that he used to love to tell us about—hitching trains to the Chicago World fair in 1933 and drinking liver-poisoning bootleg liquor. Dad's *Phi Gam* fraternity brothers taught him to drive a car around the campus with hand signals on his thigh, and they would do it to freak everyone out. Daddy was loud and definite about who he was, or who he thought he was, and what he wanted, snarling at the world when it tumbled him, raving at it when it cheated him, embracing it in those rare moments when he was not having a fight with it. I think he believed I would avenge the fight somehow, being the first-born and being like him, a musician and a stranger to a part of the everyday, common world that was his enemy.

Among all the old letters and year-books, school papers and old birthday cards which my mother has kept, there is a cluttered assortment of pictures of me, my brothers and my sister through the years. In one I am a baby, just three months old; in another I am by the car in my short pants helping my father wash the old Buick with the hose from the backyard; there is one of me in the arms of my great grandfather Booth. In one, I am sitting on top of a table covered with poker chips and my eyes are as big and as round as the chips themselves.

I remember all kinds of fleeting, vivid moments when I see those pictures. I remember the time, when I was six, that I rode my new purple bicycle down the street with no panties on. Somebody saw me and told my mother and I got my bottom spanked. One day I rode over to a friend's house and we went to a store to steal that plastic stuff that you blow through a long tube to make bubbles. We went in the store and acted real nonchalant about things. The store people were decorating the window, and everyone was laughing at something. We started to laugh, too, to cover up the fact that we were going to steal the stuff. I put a tube and a blower into my pocket and pulled my shirt down over it. My friend did the same thing. We walked around the store some more, and pretended to be really interested in what was happening. When we were going to leave, we bought some bubble gum to look like we had a reason to come in there; the lady took my money and said, "Honey, what's in your pocket?" I think that I almost died on the spot. I showed her, and she took our names and our phone numbers and said she was going to call our parents and tell them about it. We were seven and inexperienced thieves, and gave her our right phone numbers, and I lived in perpetual fear for two weeks afterwards, but the lady never called.

I used to go up the block to catch butterflies in a big glass refrigerator jar. There were all kinds of butterflies that came to light on the bushes they have in California that look a little like sweet william plants; I would get the jar good and full of beautiful butterflies, and on the way home I would usually drop the jar and it would break and all the butterflies would fly away. I had braids then and some of my friends said one day, "Why don't we play shoot the arrow through Judy's braids?" They shot, and one of the arrows hit me just below the eye; a little closer would have been too close. I ran home, with the cut bleeding, and told my mother that I fell down on a bottle.

There was a home for boys from broken families up the street from our house. It was called the Lark Ellen Home for Boys. My first date was with one of the boys. I was eight. We went to a Halloween party up in the mountains. We rode there in a big open truck, and on the way home my boyfriend said, "Close your eyes, I am going to do something special to you." He kissed me on the mouth and said, "Do you know what that was?" I said, "No." I don't think he asked me out again.

There are pictures of my brothers and sisters and me through the years: Michael four years younger than me, displaying the sweet beautiful Michael-smile from behind his glasses while he plays the trumpet. Michael, who wanted, on his third birthday, only one thing. A rose bush. Mama got it for him and he loved it. He took care of it and used to go and stand by it near the picket-fence where it blossomed peach-colored roses all the five years we lived in Los Angeles. David, under the Christmas tree, tow-headed and grinning, used to fall asleep in his high chair when he was a baby, and he still falls asleep, calm and peaceful in the middle of any storm. Denver John, suave, long haired and smiling that invincible smile as in the family pictures of our brother Michael's wedding.

I want to tease Mama sometimes about having given birth to a city. We had just moved to Denver, when Denver-John was born, and it was my father who named him Denver. I wrote a poem once about a lady who fantasizes that her son is a city full of winding streets and endless harbors, stores full of sweets, museums and cathedrals, and insurrections led by fist-waving students. There is Holly Ann, the baby of our family, beautiful, the only brown-eyed Collins. Holly Ann, so close to me, who travelled to Russia and Poland with me. She is no longer the baby I took care of when I was 14, but almost a woman herself now. Holly Ann's face retains throughout the years that clarity of really being there. My own face, as a child, has some distant and filtered quality, as though I wasn't sure whether I might not disappear at any moment. There I am, standing in a field of alfalfa next to the cows at my great-grandfather's farm in Idaho; and sitting naked at three, having a bath in a big round pan in the yard, or standing by the tulips with my feet crossed and my tight braids pulling. I still squint like I do in those pictures and my cheeks curl up and my eyes water.

I remember a lot about my great-grandfather's farm, more than about most places. I would help my great-grandmother make sugar-cookies while sitting on a tall stool in the big kitchen next to the iron stove. There, outside the window, the pastures stood solemn green forever. There was the "separating room" where the fresh milk was brought in huge tins and dumped steaming into the top of the separator, and the whole place smelled of cheese and sweet butter. I always wandered in and out of the doors of the farmhouse. Up the dirt road on the way into town I made friends with a billy goat who was tied to the fence. This child of my memory of childhood, found some peace there on the farm, with the bright green grass and the good, warm smells, and the old, kind people.

I loved my great-grandparents and I remember the sorrow I felt when I began to realize that they were very, very old, older than anybody I could imagine and that soon they would be no more. For three years great-grandfather took care of great-grandma after she was paralyzed by a stroke. They moved into town from the farm. The day after grandma died he cut the cover photo off *Life Magazine,* a picture of Pier Angeli, and put it on the pillow where she had slept beside him for so many years. It seemed that he was the oldest man in the world by then. He would come limping with his cane to his daughter's house to eat his supper. Afterwards my mother would say, "Won't you sit a while, Granddad?" And he would say: "No, Marge, I have to go home and take care of my girl." And he would limp slowly back home and sit and rock and stare at the picture of the girl who looked so much like Bell Booth when she was young, the bride of the young Mr. Booth. There is a song that reminds me of them. It is Jacques Brel's song "Les Vieux," The Old People. The chorus of it goes: "The old clock in the parlor that says yes, that says no, that says I wait for you; The old clock in the parlor that says yes, that says no, that waits for us all."

When I was ten I started studying piano with Dr. Brico in Denver. She lived in a brownstone house that always smelled of grapefruit and rosin. Her studio, around the corner in the same building, was a massive room with two grand pianos in it, both Steinways, and one with Tchaikovsky's name imprinted on the sound board. The photographs on the wall are of her friends; "To Antonia with Love," "To Antonia with many fond wishes from her grateful student," "To Antonia with affectionate regards from Sibelius." She studied conducting with Sibelius when she was a young woman. She conducted his orchestra in Finland on his 82nd birthday. She visited Schweitzer every summer in Lambaréné, Africa, and while the nurses tended the African patients and the big tarantulas crawled slowly through the make-shift hospital compound in the tropical heat, Dr. Brico and Schweitzer played Bach and studied the great master's work on an organ. There are photographs of "Antonia and Albert" in the jungle smiling and wearing white jungle helmets to keep their graying heads from the sunlight.

I called her Dr. Grico for a long time. It reminded me of Greig. I was totally in awe of her. She wore long black skirts and conducted the Businessmen's Orchestra of Denver. She cut my nails every time I came to a lesson. Right down to the quick. Sometimes she had a tray of breakfast or lunch when I came for my lesson. I loved to watch her eat. Her apples and grapefruit were always sliced into sections carefully arranged on the plate. She held the glass of fresh orange juice as if there were no surface between her hand and the juice. She would say, "Let's hear the Chopin," or "Let's play the Beethoven," and I would watch her hands reach for the music and turn the pages. She has the most beautiful hands I have ever seen. They are huge and smooth and strong. The fingers are long and the veins are all in the right places, like a Rodin sculpture. There were busts and manuscripts of all the great composers and conductors. They hung and stood around the room, intimidating me; and Sibelius, Mozart, Beethoven all looked like Dr. Brico to me. She has a long complicated imposing nose on her heavy-boned Dutch face. Her hair is tousled, rising in gray curls from her head. Her eyes looked at me full of reproach for the unmemorized Schumann and the clumsy Bach, and all the eyes in the pictures and bronze faces looked at me too. Their faces were full of sadness sometimes because I was such a lazy student, and their eyes said they wouldn't worry about me at all except that I was so talented, they nodded agreement, and shouldn't waste my gift.

I play this with a Travis style pick, in a regular tuning.

a maid of constant sorrow

Words and Music Traditional

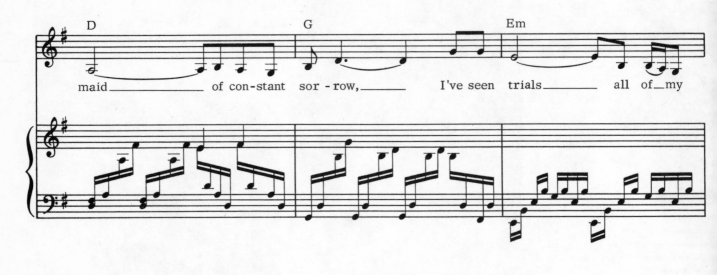

2. Your friends may say that I'm a stranger,
   My face they'll never see no more.
   There is just one promise that's given,
   I'll sail on God's golden shore.

3. All through this world I'm bound to ramble,
   Through sun and wind and drivin' rain,
   I'm bound to ride the western railway,
   Perhaps I'll take the very next train.

4. I am a maid of constant sorrow,
   I've seen trials all of my days.
   I'm going back to California,
   Place where I was partly raised.

*In England and Ireland, where everyone
knows this song, you have only to begin it in a club to have a full chorus of harmony;
I end concerts with it acappella, and people know it here now almost as well
as they do there.*

THE WILD MOUNTAIN THYME

**Words and Music Traditional
Adapted by Francis McPeake**

1. For the sum-mer-time is com-ing, And the trees are sweet-ly
2. If my true love will not go, I will sure-ly find an-
3. I will build my love a bow-er By yon clear crys-tal

bloom-ing, And the wild moun-tain thyme, Blooms a-round the pur-ple
oth-er, To pull wild moun-tain thyme, All a-round the pur-ple
foun-tain, And in it I will pile All the flow-ers from the

heath-er.
heath-er. Will you go, lad-die, go?
moun-tain.

Refrain With a steady rhythm

And we'll all go to-geth-er, To pull

wild moun-tain thyme,___ All a - round the pur-ple

heath-er.___ Will you__ go, lad - die,___

go?_____ go?_____

Oh, Hamilton Camp how you sing
this song to make the heart break and the past live.

BOLD FENIAN MAN

Slowly, freely

(Guitar tacet)

Words and Music Traditional

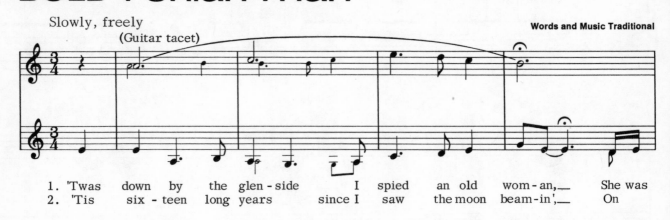

1. 'Twas down by the glen - side I spied an old wom - an,___ She was
2. 'Tis six - teen long years since I saw the moon beam - in',___ On

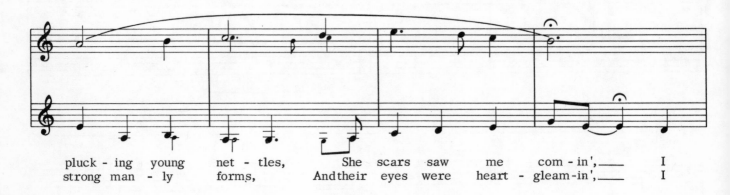

pluck - ing young net - tles, She scars saw me com - in',___ I
strong man - ly forms, And their eyes were heart - gleam - in',___ I

lis - tened a - while to the song she was hum - min'___ } Glo - ry, O, glo - ry,
see them all now, sure, in all my day - dream - in'___ }

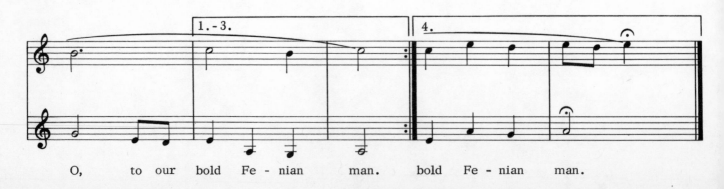

1. - 3.

4.

O, to our bold Fe - nian man. bold Fe - nian man.

3. Some died on the hillside,
   Some died with a stranger,
   And wise men have judged
   That their cause was a failure.
   They fought for their freedom
   And they never feared danger—
   Glory, O, glory, O,
   To our bold Fenian man.

4. I passed on my way,
   Thanks to God that I met her.
   Be life long or short
   I'll never forget her.
   There may have been brave men
   But there'll never be better—
   Glory, O, glory, O,
   To our bold Fenian man.

If you want to do this like it is on my record, tune the sixth
String to D, and capo up two frets. That puts your E chord in the D position.

JOHN RILEY

Words and Music by Ricky Neff and Bob Gibson

Lively, flowing

1. A fair young maid _____ was in her gar - den, _____ Strange young man _____ came rid - ing by; _____ He said, "Fair maid, _____ will you mar - ry me?" And

23

2. Oh, no, kind sir, I cannot marry thee
For I've a lad and he sails the sea,
Though he's been gone for seven years,
Still he will return to me.

3. Well, what if he's in some battle slain,
Or if he's drowned in the deep salt sea?
Or what if he's found another love,
And he and his love, both married be?

4. If he is in some battle slain
Then I shall die when the moon doth wane;
And if he's drowned in the deep salt sea,
Still I'm true to his memory, and

5. If he's found another love,
And he and his love both married be;
I wish them health and happiness
Where they live across the sea.

6. He picked her up in his arms so strong
And kisses he gave her one, two, three,
Saying, "Weep no more my own true love,
I am your long lost John Riley."
Saying, "Weep no more my own true love,
I am your long lost John Riley."

Cynthia Gooding sings a great acapella version of this on an Elektra album called 'Faithful Lovers and other Phenomena.'

THE GREAT SILKIE

Words Traditional   Music by James Waters

Moderately, with mournful mystery

1. In Nor - way there sits___ a maid,___ "By'e - loo my ba - by"___ she be - gins,___ "Lit - tle know I, my
2. Then there___ a - rose at her bed's feet___ Ane grum - ley guest, I'm sure it was he,___ •Sayin' "Here___ am I, they

3. I am a man upon the land
   And I am a silkie in the sea.
   And when I am in my own country
   My dwellin' is in Shule Skerry.

4. Then he has taken a purse of gold
   And he has put it upon her knee,
   Saying, "Give to me my little wee son,
   And take thee up thy nurse's fee.

5. "And it shall come to pass on a summer day
   When the sun shines hot on ev'ry stone.
   That I shall take my little wee son
   And I'll teach him for to swim in the foam."

6. "And you will marry a gunner good,
   And a proud good gunner I'm sure he'll be,
   And he'll go out on a May morning
   And he'll kill both my young son and me."

7. And lo, she did marry a gunner good,
   And a proud good gunner I'm sure it was he,
   And the very first shot that he did shoot
   He killed the son and the Great Silkie.

8. *Repeat 1st verse.*

What a great song this is, sung acapella!

THE WARS OF GERMANY

Words and Music Traditional

Slow march

1. Oh woe be to the__ or-ders__ that marched my love__ a-way, And__ woe be to the bit-ter tears I shed up-on this day; And woe be to the blood-y wars of

3. Oh, woe be to the orders
That marched my love away,
And woe be to the bitter tears
I shed upon this day;

And woe be to the country
Where our men are forced to be
And woe be to the foreign war
That stole my love from me.

THE CROW ON THE CRADLE

Gently, but with bitter irony

Words and Music by Sidney Carter

The sheep's in the mead - ow, the cow's in the corn; Now is the time for a child to be born. You'll cry at the

moon and you'll laugh at the sun; If he's a boy he'll

car - ry a gun, Sang the crow on the cra - dle.

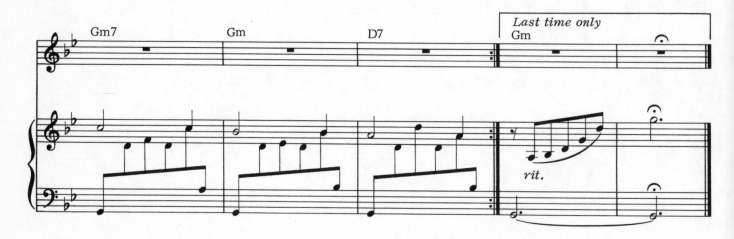

2. If it should be that our baby's a girl
   Never you mind if her hair doesn't curl.
   Rings on her fingers, bells on her toes!
   A bomber above her wherever she goes,
   Sang the crow on the cradle.

3. Rockabye baby, the dark and the light!
   Somebody's baby is born for a fight.
   Rockabye baby, the white and the black!
   Somebody's baby is not coming back,
   Sang the crow on the cradle.

4. Your Mother and Father they'll scrape and they'll save!
   Build you a coffin, and dig you a grave.
   Hushabye little one, why do you weep?
   We have a toy that will put you to sleep,
   Sang the crow on the cradle.

5. Bring me a gun and I'll shoot that bird dead!
   That's what your Mother and Father once said.
   Crow on the cradle, what shall I do?
   That is the fate I leave up to you,
   Sang the crow on the cradle.

GOLDEN APPLES OF THE SUN

Words by William Butler Yeats
Music Traditional

And hooked a ber-ry to a thread.

And when white moths were on the wing

And moth-like stars were flick-'ring out

I dropped the ber-ry in a stream

And caught a lit-tle

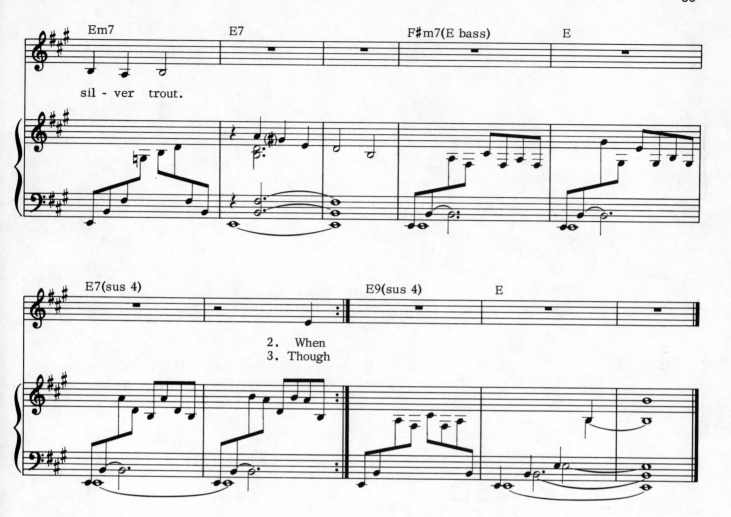

sil - ver trout.

2. When
3. Though

2. When I had laid it on the ground
   And gone to blow the fire aflame
   Something rustled on the ground
   And someone called me by my name
   It had become a glimmering girl—
   With apple blossoms in her hair—
   Who called me by my name and ran
   And vanished in the bright'ning air.

3. Though I am old with wandering
   Through hollow lands and hilly lands
   I will find out where she has gone
   And kiss her lips and take her hand
   And walk through long green dappled grass
   And pluck till time and times are done
   The silver apples of the moon
   The golden apples of the sun.

Part 2

One night fifteen years ago, in the Rocky Mountains, in a log cabin high above Denver under a pouring rain, the fire was burning bright and the songs filled the room with a nostalgia so deep and embracing you could hold it around you like a shawl, like a woolen comforter, like a fur rug. The farther into the night we went, the more beautiful the music and the more songs of Woody Guthrie we remembered, half-remembered, here a verse, there a whole chorus. Marty Hoffman sang "This Land is Your Land," and by the time I had another jug of homebrew I knew the chorus, and then the verses, and I thought it was the most beautiful song I had ever heard. Mart had one of those voices that makes you think back into your own life; anyway, he was one of the best singers I ever heard. He wrote the melody to another of Woody's songs, called "Deportees." The sound of the rain stopped. The air grew quiet. Our worlds were silent now, our voices hung in the stillness of the room. The sun started to rise out over the vast plains, up out of the miles of flat, flat prairie that stretches from the Rockies into Kansas. The light filled the log-walled room, and still we sat watching the fire die and dreaming the dreams that the songs gave us.

Now, years later, Marty Hoffman is out in Arizona working on an Indian reservation and Dick Barker is running float trips down the Snake River in the Grand Teton National Park. Nancy Burton is married and more beautiful than ever. She lives in Tucson where the sunsets are vivid. Lingo the Drifter is drifting somewhere with pine twigs in his hat and a dark blazing look in his eyes that reminds me of Dick Fariña's. We were drifters all, but those moments hold like interwoven vines across the distant years. Our feelings for each other were strong and intertwined; we shared moments, songs, country evenings. From these friends I learned my first folk songs.

I was drawn, in those days, to the saddest and most poignant of the songs I heard and the songs about my own heredity, the songs of Ireland and England and Scotland, the songs of Woody Guthrie, the ballads of the Western cowboy, the songs of the American settlers. I wanted to know where I came from, who my people were, what things they thought about after the crops were in, after the boats came home, after the freight-loaded trains ran on up into the northwest.

When I was three and four years old my father worked for a high school touring outfit called National School Assemblies, and I lived in the back seat of a '39 Buick named Claudia. Daddy did medicine shows, as he called them, music and poetry and stories. My mother drove. From my back seat house I watched the world pass by. The stretches of Montana and Idaho, Oregon, Washington, Nevada, the earth smells and changes that the seasons brought, came to me like promises and I was content, happy to go wherever the Claudia took me. Those shadowy people, my grandfathers and grandfathers' fathers, trainmen and explorers, Admiral Byrd on my mother's side, were all part of that land and they are the people the music told me about.

When I finished high school I wandered about vaguely for a year, working in a guest ranch in the mountains for the summer. I had a scholarship in the fall to a college in Illinois called Macmurray. I will never know why they chose to give me a scholarship. I suspected for some time that it was punishment. I was way out in the midwest, far from Colorado, far from home. My friend Pat Noonan and I took the train back to Denver on holidays and I always brought out the guitar and sang in the club car. I gathered songs and dreamed in melancholy through an Illinois winter and finally returned in the spring to Denver. There, home again, I married my high school sweetheart.

When Peter and I were first together we left Denver and headed for the mountains. We stayed in my god-father's cabin near Estes Park and I fiddled around with the wood stove, learning to make it do what I wanted it to do. Pete went into town every day to find us work for the summer. One afternoon, he came back to the cabin and said, "You won't believe it . . . I found the perfect job." And so he had. A lodge, back in the wilderness of Rocky Mountain National Park: they needed a couple to run it for the summer. The people who owned it lived at Bear Lake Lodge in Rocky Mountain National Park, and we went up that evening to see them. We liked each other right away. Jim Bishop poured us big glasses of bourbon, told us all about his winter cattle ranch in Arizona and the history of Fern Lake Lodge. Jim was the kind of man who made you think the wild west was still in the process of being won, mostly by him. We put up in one of the cabins near Bear Lake Lodge and the next day the fat cook taught me how to bake bread. I had lied about knowing how, but I knew I could do it because I knew I could do anything I set my mind to.

We went up the mountain to Fern Lake on a bright clear June day. There isn't anything like those mountains. We both carried heavy packs, with enough food to last five or six days—until the pack horse would be over with our first load of supplies, the guitar and a bottle of Jim Beam. We were really on our own until then. The trail starts up alongside Bear Lake. The land is dry on this side and rocky, full of low pine and scrub. The way curls up steeply circling and winding to the top of the first mountain, then, stretching out above, the deeply-wooded, wild, alpine-like terrain begins on the other side of Bear Lake.

Some day I will write a book about that summer. Peter and I lived in the high alpine lake region near the timberline in Rocky Mountain National Park, running the lodge called Fern Lake Lodge, a four and a half mile hike from the nearest road. I baked bread and pies on the wood stove. We had the whole range of mountains and lakes and sky and stars to ourselves after the last hiker had descended to city in the afternoon. Late evening was for fishing, talking by the fire. Friends came to visit, hikers from all over the country. One night we listened to my father, so proud to have made that hike and climbed that height. He described, with his fingers running over the logs, how our puncheon floor was made: how logs are cut to about six inch lengths, stood on end side by side, and the spaces filled with tar. It is hell to keep clean. My father was the only one to see that floor at the lodge and know what it was. We would sing songs with a close friend who might have stayed overnight after hiking up the mountain bringing fresh avocados and Mexican beer, a journey of love with a heavy pack. The horse brought supplies in once a week and my guitar managed to make the first pack trip.

It was surprising to me how many of these people hiking in the wilderness remembered the songs they learned as children in Europe or in college, in the folk music revival, as it was called then. In those mountains, we were visited by travelers who bore songs like gifts and traded the weight of their packs for lyric melodies and stories of the world.

Up in the tundra above Fern Lake amidst the waterfalls from the glaciers and the myriad tiny alpine flowers that grow above the timberline in the spring, my brothers took my father's ashes last summer and let them loose close to the sun.

After our summer in the mountains at Fern Lake Lodge my stomach began to grow bigger and bigger with my baby, who started kicking and demanding more room in my bed, in my clothes, in my mind. We moved down to Boulder and rented a basement apartment. Peter got a job driving a truck and registered for school. I worked at the University during registration, getting bigger all the time till my stomach was the first thing people actually saw upon entering the Halls of Ivy. My guitar sat out on my stomach when I sang and I had trouble getting close enough to the stove to cook.

I took a typing course at the University for a while, growing further and further away from the typing table as the weeks went by. Peter and I read books on babies, turning the pages and smiling furtively at each other late at night after he had finished studying. The doctor poked and smiled and proudly told me my son was going to be big, yes, and healthy. He said nothing about red hair, but then I wouldn't have thought to ask. I think I really liked being pregnant. The memory of it is all soft and taken care of, inside and outside.

One night in January, the sign came that the child in there with wiggling fists and feet and the strong heartbeat, who had never even given me morning sickness, was about to fight his way out. We drove in the snow storm to the hospital in our old green Plymouth, in the middle of the night. He was big, nine pounds and two ounces, and I delivered him after 28 hours of labor, with two doctors tugging away with forceps against his little cheeks. He came out finally, yelling, triumphant. Clark had strawberry silk hair and blue eyes and two forceps marks around his cheeks for a while, and he was the most beautiful baby I have ever seen, even to this day. On the eighth day of the month of January he fought his way into the world of the snow-covered winter mountains of Colorado and the warm little apartment under Mrs. Tingley's house where Judy and Peter lived.

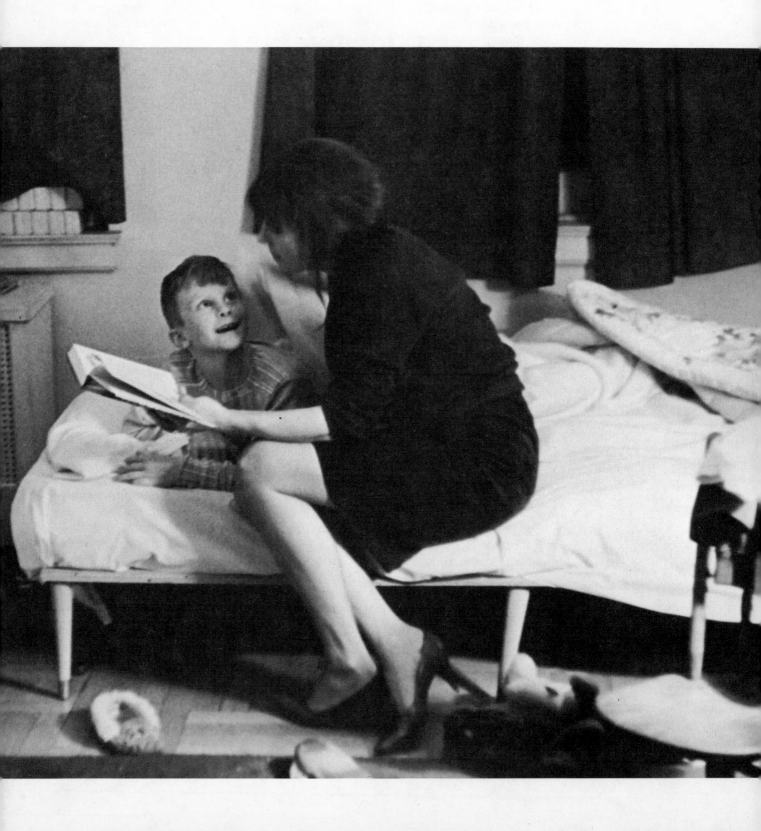

anathea

Words by Neil Roth   Music by Lydia Wood

La

La _____   La _____

Last time only

Fine

Laz - lo Feh-er stole a stal - lion, Stole him from the mist - y moun - tain

And they chased him and they caught him,___

And in i - ron chains they bound him.___

(*Last time D.C. al Fine*)

2. Word was brought to Anathea
   That her brother was in prison.
   "Bring me gold and six fine horses,
   I will buy my brother's freedom."

3. "Judge, oh, judge, please spare my brother,
   I will give you gold and silver."
   "I don't want your gold and silver,
   All I want are your sweet favours."

4. "Anathea, oh, my sister,
   Are you mad with grief and sorrow?
   He will rob you of your flower,
   And he'll hang me from the gallows.

5. Anathea did not heed him,
   Straight way to the judge went running.
   In his golden bed at midnight,
   There she heard the gallows groaning.

6. "Cursed be that judge so cruel,
   Thirteen years may he lie bleeding.
   Thirteen doctors cannot cure him,
   Thirteen shelves of drugs can't heal him.

7. "Anathea, Anathea,
   Don't go out into the forest.
   There among the green pines standing,
   You will find your brother hanging."

Ten O'Clock, All is Well

The Town Crier's Song

Words and Music by Bob Camp and Bob Gibson

Slow and steady

1. Ten o'-clock, all's well, Ten o'-clock, all's well,

Town cri-er call-ing, swing-in' his bell, Ten o'-clock, all's well,

Ex-cept for the girl with the tear___ in her eye, Whose sail-or had left ___with a

bit - ter good - bye. He swore on his life they nev - er would part, But

he sailed and he left___ with her heart. drowned.___

46

Refrain:
Eleven o'clock, all's well,
Eleven o'clock, all's well,
Town Crier callin', swingin' his bell,
Eleven o'clock, all's well.

2. Oh, where were her words when he turned to go?
Of the new life within her now he'd never know.
She walked through the night full of grief and despair,
Cryin' why has he gone and where?

Refrain:
Twelve o'clock, all's well,
Twelve o'clock, all's well,
Town Crier callin', swingin' his bell,
Twelve o'clock, all's well.

3. She thought of her man who had sailed away,
Not even a kiss when he left that day.
She walked to the dock where the sea meets the town,
And she stepped from the shore and she drowned.

THE DOVE

Words by Ewan McColl   Music Traditional

The dove she is a pret-ty bird, She sings as she flies, She

brings us glad ti - dings and tells us no lies. _____

2. Come all you young fellows, take warning by me,
   Don't go for a soldier, don't join no army.
   For the dove she will leave you, the raven will come,
   And death will come marching at the beat of the drum.

3. Come all you pretty fair maids, come walk in the sun,
   And don't let your young man ever carry a gun,
   For the gun it will scare her, and she'll fly away,
   And then there'll be weeping by night and by day.

4. The dove she is a pretty bird, she sings as she flies.
   She brings us glad tidings, and tells us no lies.
   She drinks the spring waters to make her voice clear
   When her nest she is building and the summer is near.

IN THE HILLS OF SHILOH

Words by Shel Silverstein   Music by Jim Friedman

Slowly
(Guitar tacet)

1. Have you seen A - man - da Blaine in the hills of Shi - loh,
Wan - d'rin' in the morn - ing rain through the hills of Shi - loh,

Have you seen her at her door lis - t'nin' for the can - non's roar,

And a man who went to war from the hills of Shi - loh?

2. Have you heard her mourn - ful cries in the hills of Shi - loh?
Have you seen her haunt - ed eyes in the hills of Shi - loh?

Have you seen her run - ning down, search - ing through the sleep - ing town,

In a yel - lowed wed - ding gown, in the hills of Shi - loh?

3. Have you seen her stand - ing there in the hills of Shi - loh,
   Wind a - blow - ing through her hair in the hills of Shi - loh?

Lis - t'ning for the sound of guns, lis - t'ning for the roll - ing drums.

And a man who nev - er comes to the hills of Shi - loh.

4. Have you heard A - man - da sing in the hills of Shi - loh,
Whis-p'ring to her wed - ding ring in the hills of Shi - loh?

Hear her hum - ming soft and low; poor A - man - da does - n't know 'twas

end - ed for - ty years a - go in the hills of Shi - loh.

*For this song that has endured
so long I thank you, Pete Seeger, and for your unswerving faith
that love can bring peace to the world of men.*

Turn! Turn! Turn!

Words from the Book of Ecclesiastes   Adapted—Music by Pete Seeger

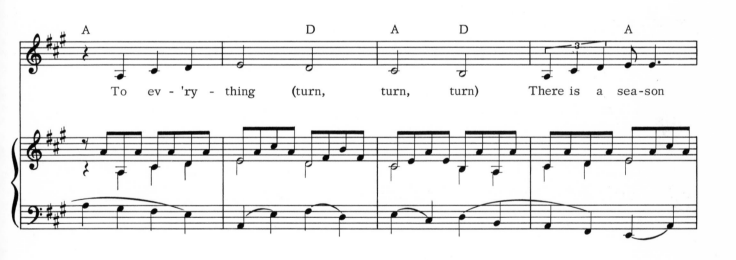

To ev - 'ry - thing (turn,   turn,   turn) There is a sea-son

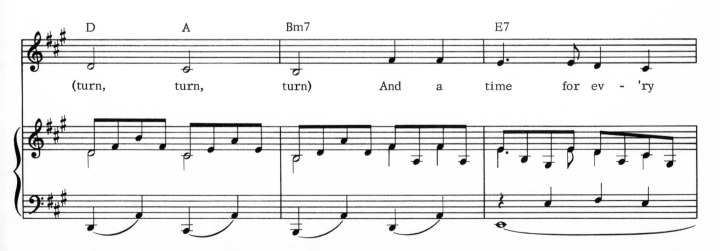

(turn,   turn,   turn) And a time for ev - 'ry

52

Chorus:
To ev'ry thing (turn, turn, turn)
There is a season (turn, turn, turn)
And a time for ev'ry purpose under heaven.

2. A time to build up, a time to break down;
   A time to dance, a time to mourn;
   A time to cast away stones, a time to gather stones together.
   Chorus

3. A time of love, a time of hate;
   A time of war, a time of peace;
   A time you may embrace, a time to refrain from embracing.
   Chorus

4. A time to gain, a time to lose;
   A time to rend, a time to sew;
   A time to love, a time to hate; a time of peace, I swear it's not too late.
   Chorus—repeat last line

Today the migrant workers
in all parts of our country strive for a decent life,
a living wage, an answer to who makes the rich landowners rich.

Deportee
Plane Wreck at Los Gatos

Words by Woody Guthrie   Music by Martin Hoffman

Moderately

The crops are all in and the peach-es are rot - ting,

The or - an-ges piled in their cre - o - sote

dumps; You're fly - ing 'em back to the Mex - i - can

56

2. My father's own father, he waded that river,
   They took all the money he made in his life;
   My sisters and brothers come work in the fruit fields.
   Rode that truck till they went down and died.

3. Some of us are illegal, and others not wanted,
   Our work contract's out and we have to move on;
   Six hundred miles to that Mexican border,
   They chased us like rustlers, like outlaws, like thieves.

   Chorus:
   Goodbye to my Juan, goodbye Rosalita,
   Adios, mis amigos, Jesus y Maria,
   You won't have a name when you ride the big airplane
   All they will call you will be deportee.

4. The sky plane caught fire over Los Gatos canyon,
   A fireball of lightning, and shook all our hills,
   Who are all these dear friends, all scattered like dry leaves?
   The radio says they are just deportees.

5. Is this the best way we can raise our good orchards?
   Is this the best way we can grow our good crops?
   To die and be scattered to rot on the topsoil,
   To be called by no name except deportees?
   Chorus twice

In London, in Albert Hall
I sang this after the Aberfan tragedy;
it was clear that the bells do not always ring with joy.

THE BELLS OF RHYMNEY

Words by Idris Davies   Music by Pete Seeger

Oh___ what will you give me?___ say the
sad bells of Rhym - ney,   Is there hope for the fu - ture?

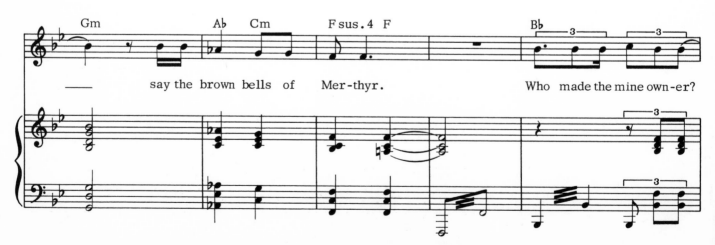

___ say the brown bells of Mer-thyr.   Who made the mine own-er?

Part 3

after Clark was born, the winter grew cold. One night it was snowing hard and Peter had to get up at five in the morning to go to work before classes. It was freezing. The wind was blowing the snow under the front door. It was still dark. I was feeding Clark breakfast and Peter said, "Wouldn't it be a great idea for you to get a job singing?"

It was an idea and, later, I went down to the local beer club called Michael's Pub, and auditioned for the man who owned it, Mike Bessessi. Dear Mike, he really was good to me, and although he told me right off he hated folk music and was hiring me only because he could make money with it, he was very kind. He paid me a hundred dollars a week. It was like a gold mine to us, then. He threw in all the beer I could drink and later, after a while, he told me that he really loved what I was doing.

Peter quit his winter morning job with the paper service, and I began my career singing to the college students who drank pitchers of watery 3.2 beer and listened as if they were dazed. I used to drive our old Plymouth down to work five nights a week, starting at eight and ending at twelve. I sang songs like "The Great Silkie" and "The Three Marys" and "Ten Thousand Goddamned Cattle" and "If You've Never Made Love to the Landlady's Daughter then You Cannot Have Another Piece of Pie" and "The Sirie Peaks"—a song about two cowboys who go to town and get drunk and on the way back to the ranch they run into the devil and tie knots in his tail. After work at midnight, I would drink some awful beer with Mike and my friends and hurry home in the green Plymouth, through the quiet streets of Boulder under the stars and the rock-faced flatiron mountains that rise into the Rockies. Sometimes it snowed, sometimes it was very cold, and sometimes I would lose my voice from singing too much. Back in our basement my baby gurgled and smiled and grew and at night when I worked Peter stayed home with him and studied. My reputation was spreading and reached a man who offered me a better job, not in the lewd nightclub he ran in Denver, but in a tourist trap in Central City, a second act to a rock and roll band. I took it. I got a twenty-five dollar raise. I put on leotards and pointed shoes and a red silk shirt and became the local troubadour at the Gilded Garter. It was the summer of 1959 and I was 19 years old.

I had to sing six nights a week in Central City in the mountains. For a while, I got a job in the daytime, too, helping the cook across the street in the Old Glory Hole Restaurant put up the lunches. All week long I would sing at the Garter, usually until two in the morning, and on Sunday nights I was off. Peter worked in a gas station.

On Sunday afternoons, the tourists would peer into the gilded front door of the Garter and fill their mouths with popcorn and tacos, and listen. They would wander in and stare at me and at each other warily and maybe slip into a back booth, husband and wife, while the kids milled around the doors and the bar in the strange inside light of a Sunday afternoon. Sometimes they would come to me after the show and say, "You know, I haven't heard songs like that in years. What kind of songs are they? Are they Country and Western songs?"

That summer, Peter and Clark and I rose from basement level in Boulder, to the second story of a rickety old house in Blackhawk, about a mile down the hill from Central City. The whole area has been gutted of its ore, the mountains eaten out whole and their insides strewn across the brown hills, covering the mountains with black and silver sand that glitters on bright days. The city above Blackhawk was the city of Haw Tabor and Baby Doe Tabor, his daughter. He called her Silver Dollar; and in the days of their glory in the 1840's, Central City was a contrast of wealth, and of the blood, sweat and tears of the silver miners who sometimes struck it rich, and sometimes whittled away their lives washing thimbles-full of gold and silver from the puny river beds, living, after the rush, in cardboard and tin shacks along the canyon, their mangy dogs low slung and hungry all winter. There are still a few old timers left on the road up to Central, along the Canon River, standing off without smiles, watching the cars go by with still eyes, like sentinels from the old days. But where the lights were shining back then was the city Haw Tabor built out of the wealth of that mad search. It was culture, pouring out of the dark mountains and onto the vast plains of Colorado. Men smelled it miles off, in the valleys of Louisiana and the eastern seaboard states, and they came, lured to the great silver fields. Haw Tabor's opera house burned bright and clear and the candles and silk and perfume from France beckoned like pools of liquid silver in the dark ore-laden Rockies. The men came and the silver went out and the big tins of cheese and fine bourbon in barrels and cigars from strange lands came up the tough dirt roads from Denver along with the trimmings, the girls. The ladies came to help the boys stay happy away from Louisiana and Boston, away from their homes out in the lonesome west. In a big church-like house on a hill outside Central City there is still the balcony where the whores had to sit, to keep the town gentry free from guilt by association on Sundays. They did the singing, from up there on the balcony, singing the hymns from the old days. The night I visited the house, now restored in perfect dirt-floored condition, I had a vision they were watching over me, those ladies of the dark silver nights, who comforted the men who lived and loved in the town that the Tabors built. The ladies of Denver did culture a service some years ago by restoring most of the town, and it is the thing now to ride up on a Sunday and traipse up and down the sidewalks staring at the few sturdy locals or the transients, like I was, buying little paper-back books on the minerals and wildflowers of Colorado, swinging through the doors of the Old Glory Hole Bar, looking at the odd tools and mirrors and dusty hand-wrought western gear that belonged to the men who chiselled out some comfort in the rugged west. At night after I sang I would wander around sometimes, maybe meet Terry Williams and his wife Nancy or Lou Cady in one of the mining bars up the street toward the opera house; and I often felt the presence of those departed silver searchers all around me.

Across the dirt road from our house in Blackhawk, there was a big ware-house with a Bull Durham sign painted in red and yellow on the roof. That was the view, with the rusty river beyond and the big green hills on the other side of the abandoned, desolated mines.

Clark was crawling by then, hunting, grabbing fingers, grinning and eating and growing. I would sometimes carry him in a pack on my back when I went to town to shop. He and I went to Boulder to do the laundry, over to Denver to visit my folks. I sang songs of western love and lore to the tourists, and I began to be aware of a turmoil and struggle somewhere deep inside of me. But I was happy there. It was still the rough old west.

It is a miracle how a song
finds its way thru the chaos to give us simplicity.

WINTER SKY

Words and Music Billy Edd Wheeler

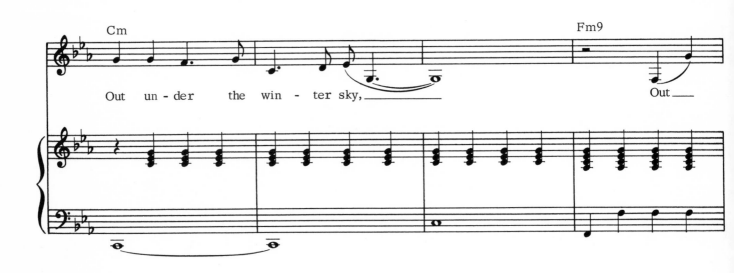

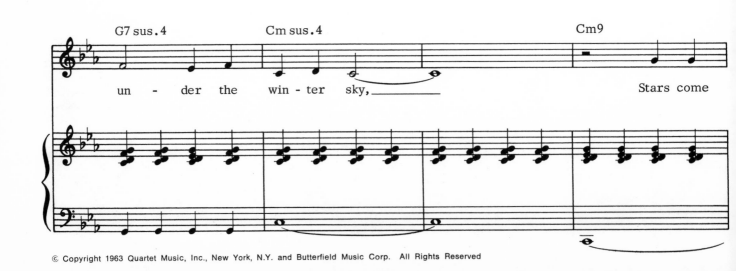

Tom is a rare man; to write a good love song is something,
to write a funny, hard-hitting protest song is something—to do both is amazing.

THE LAST THING ON MY MIND

With motion, but quietly

Words and Music by Tom Paxton

It's a

les - son too late   for   the   learn - ing,   made of

sand, made of sand. In the wink of an eye my soul is turn-ing___ in your hand, in your hand.

Chorus

Are you go - ing a - way with no word of fare - well?

Will there be___ not a trace left be - hind? Well, I

2. As we walk on, my thoughts keep a-tumblin',
   'Round and 'round, 'round and 'round.
   Underneath our feet the subway's rumblin',
   Underground, underground.

3. You got reasons a-plenty for goin',
   This I know, this I know.
   For the weeks have been steadily growin',
   Please don't go, please don't go.
   Chorus twice

One night in a Detroit theatre
a stage hand told me this was the best song
he had ever heard and made me write the words out on an unrolled paper cup.

my ramBLIN' BOY

Words and Music by Tom Paxton

Easy-going tempo

Chorus

So here's to you, _____ my ram-blin'

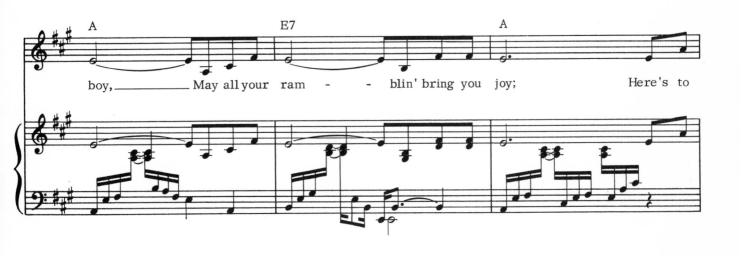

boy, _____ May all your ram - - blin' bring you joy; Here's to

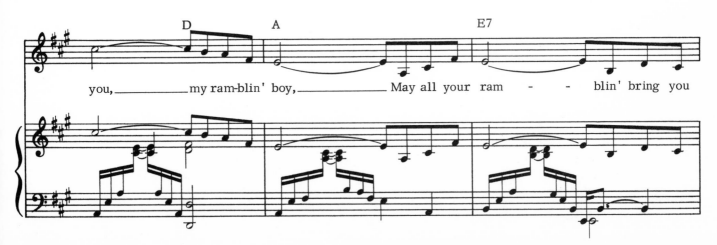

you, _____ my ram-blin' boy, _____ May all your ram - - blin' bring you

2. In Tulsa town we chanced to stray,
   We thought we'd try to work one day.
   The boss said he had room for one,
   Says my old pal, "We'd rather bum!"
   Chorus

3. Late one night in a jungle camp,
   The weather it was cold and damp.
   He got the chills and he got 'em bad.
   They took the only friend I had.
   Chorus

4. He left me here to ramble on,
   My ramblin' pal he's dead and gone.
   If when we die we go somewhere,
   I'll bet you a dollar he's ramblin' there.
   Chorus

Eric Weissberg is a wonderful musician
and a joy to work with. Between our two guitars
we made this song sound like a spring in the mountains.

THE WILD RIPPLING WATER

Words Traditional
New Arrangement by Mary Robbins

With movement, lightly

As I was a-walk-in' and a-ram-blin' one

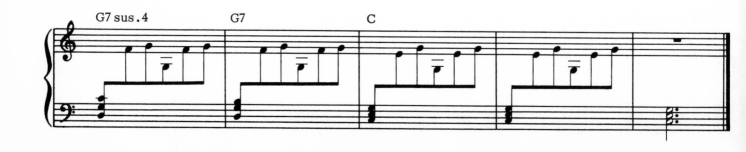

2. "Oh, where are you goin', my pretty fair maid?"
   "Just down by the river, just down by the shade,
   Just down by the river, just down by the spring,
   To see the water glidin', and the nightingale sing,
   To see the water glidin', hear the nightingale sing."

3. They had not been there but an hour or so
   When out of his satchel came fiddle and bow.
   He played a tune that made the woods ring.
   She said, "Hark, hark, hear the nightingale sing."
   She said, "Hark, hark, hear the nightingale sing."

4. He said, "Pretty lady, it's time to give o'er."
   "Oh, no, my pretty cowboy, just play one tune more.
   I'd rather hear the fiddle on the touch of one string,
   Than to see the water glidin', and the nightingale sing,
   See the wild ripplin' water, hear the nightingale sing."

5. She said, "Pretty cowboy, will you marry me?"
   "Oh no, my pretty lady, that never can be,
   I've a wife in Arizona and a lady is she.
   One wife on a cow ranch is a-plenty for me,
   One wife on a cow ranch is a-plenty for me."

6. "Well, I'm going out to Mexico, I'll stay about a year.
   I'll drink red wine, I'll drink lots of beer.
   If I ever return it will be in the spring
   To see the water glidin', and the nightingale sing,
   See the wild ripplin' water, hear the nightingale sing."

Tear Down the Walls

Rock-'n-roll style

Words and Music by Fred Nell

Tear down the walls,

Lis - ten to free-dom sing - in' out, Tear down the

82

2. Listen to the freedom ringing out,
   Tear down the walls.
   Can't you hear the church bells singing out?
   Let ev'ry man sing it over the land,
   Tear down the walls, tear down the walls.

COAL TATTOO

Fast, with bitter irony

Words and Music by Billy Edd Wheeler

1. Trav-'lin' down that coal town road; Lis-ten to my rub-ber tires whine. Good-bye to buck-eye and white syc-a-more, I'm leav-in' you be - hind. Oh__ I've been a coal man

2. Somebody said that's a strange tattoo
   You have on the side of your head.
   I said that's the mark of the number nine coal,
   A little more and I'd be dead.
   Oh, but I love the rumble and I love the dark.
   I love the cool of the slate.
   But it's going down that new road lookin' for a job,
   This trav'lin' and lookin' I hate.
   This trav'lin' and lookin' I hate.

3. I've stood for the union; walked in the line.
   Fought against the company;
   I've stood for the U. M. W. of A.
   Now who's gonna stand for me?
   Well, I got no home and I got no pay,
   Just got a worried soul.
   And this blue tattoo on the side of my head
   Left by the number nine coal.
   Left by the number nine coal.

4. Someday when I die, and go to heaven,
   Land of my dreams,
   I won't have to worry on losin' my job
   To bad times and big machines.
   Well, I got no job and I got no pay,
   Just got a worried soul,
   And this blue tattoo on the side of my head
   Left by the number nine coal.
   Left by the number nine coal.

*Chuck Israel's cello part to this song
is one of the more beautiful sounds I ever sang with. It's on the Judy Collins Concert.*

CRUEL MOTHER

Arranged and Adapted by Ewan McColl

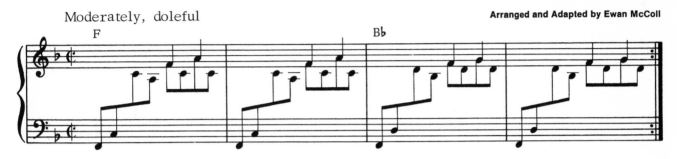

There was a

la - - dy lived in the north _____ O the rose _____

and the lin -sie O, She fell in love

with her fa - ther's clerk, Down

by the green-wood sid -ie, O!

Last time only

rit.

2. He courted her for a year and a day,
   Oh, the rose and the linsie O,
   Till her the young man did betray
   Down by the greenwood sidie, O.

3. She leaned her back up against a thorn,
   Oh, the rose and the linsie O,
   And there she had two pretty babes born
   Down by the greenwood sidie, O.

4. She took her penknife keen and sharp,
   Oh, the rose and the linsie O,
   She has stabbed it to their heart
   Down by the greenwood sidie, O.

5. As she was walking her father's hall,
   Oh, the rose and the linsie O,
   She saw two babes a-playing ball
   Down by the greenwood sidie, O.

6. She said, "Oh, babes, it's you can tell,
   Oh, the rose and the linsie O,
   What kind of death I have to die"
   Down by the greenwood sidie, O.

7. Seven years a fish in the flood,
   Oh, the rose and the linsie O,
   Seven years a bird in the wood
   Down by the greenwood sidie, O.

8. Seven years a tongue in the warning bell,
   Oh, the rose and the linsie O,
   Seven years in the flames of hell
   Down by the greenwood sidie, O.

9. Oh, welcome, welcome, fish in the flood,
   Oh, the rose and the linsie O,
   Welcome, welcome bird in the wood
   Down by the greenwood sidie, O.

10. Welcome, welcome tongue in the warning bell,
    Oh, the rose and the linsie O,
    God keep me from the flames in hell
    Down by the greenwood sidie, O.

Jim Friedman sang this to me
on a hot New York night, not so far from the Mississippi summer of 1964.

HEY, NELLY, NELLY

With excitement

Words and Music by Shel Silverstein and Jim Friedman

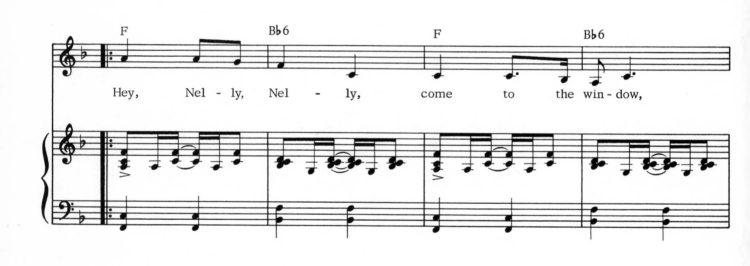

Hey, Nel - ly, Nel - ly, come to the win - dow,

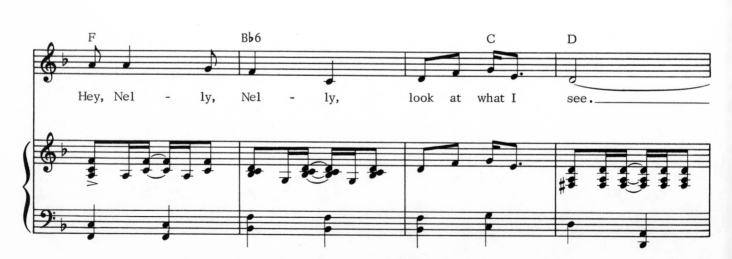

Hey, Nel - ly, Nel - ly, look at what I see.

2. Hey, Nelly, Nelly, listen what he's sayin'.
   Hey, Nelly, Nelly, he says it's gettin' late.
   And he says them black folks should all be free
   To walk around the same as you and me.
   He's talkin' 'bout a thing he calls democracy,
   And it's 1858.

3. Hey, Nelly, Nelly, hear the band a-playin'.
   Hey, Nelly, Nelly, hand me down my gun,
   'Cause the men are cheerin' and the boys are, too.
   They're all puttin' on their coats of blue.
   I can't sit around here and talk to you,
   'Cause it's 1861.

4. Hey, Nelly, Nelly, come to the window.
   Hey, Nelly, Nelly, I've come home alive.
   My coat of blue is stained with red
   And the man in the tall black hat is dead.
   We sure will remember all the things he said,
   In 1865.

5. Hey, Nelly, Nelly, come to the window.
   Hey, Nelly, Nelly, look at what I see.
   I see white folks and colored walking side by side.
   They're walkin' in a column that's a century wide.
   It's still a long and a hard and a bloody ride,
   In 1963.

Part 4

Hot Chicago, muggy . . . In 1960, we drove across the Great Plains from Denver in our funky little English Anglia and moved into a huge apartment on the South side of the Windy City, near Hyde Park. One block north was 47th street, an immense arm of the black ghetto, and one block south the slightly liberalized and integrated community of the University of Chicago.

I was hired to sing at the Gate of Horn because of a tape I made of a song called "The Great Silkie of Shule Skerry." I sent the tape to Alan Ribback, the owner. He liked it and hired me to come and sing. And there I was, dressed in my nicest, with my guitar around my neck and my leg in a cast up to my waist. I had broken it skiing in the mountains the past winter. I sang, and after that first night the cast was forgotten by all except one reviewer who commented about the second act at the Gate of Horn: a girl who hails from Aspen (which I don't; I guess he thought that was the only place they have snow in the west) and has a cast to prove it.

The Gate of Horn was eulogized years ago by Shel Silverstein, on the liner notes of an album that Bob Gibson and Hamilton Camp made there. Shel really captured the feeling of that place. The bar was separate from the club room. There I always found someone to talk to, to sip a drink with, to share the long night hours between the performances. Bob Gibson was there, leading his vague, disconnected life of love and music, and when he sang he was magic, and when he and Hamilton Camp sang together, double magic too. Hamilton Camp and I would sit in the bar and sing old Irish songs, the sweet harmonies clutching our memories, our voices wafting out into the street at the corner of Dearborn and Chicago. There is nothing there now but the old Rice Hotel. People from the Second City company were friendly with the Gate of Horn crowd, and Severn Darden was around some nights with his dark suits and his tennis shoes, benignly making the rounds of the full bar.

Alan Ribback was sailing his boat on Lake Michigan one afternoon, and ran into another boat with some friendly people on it. They started talking and before long, Alan discovered that Lord Buckley was among them. Alan asked him to work at the club. And soon, after Gibson and Camp and I had done our singing and the evening was waning into the easiness of Chicago nights, Lord Buckley would do the late last show. Most of us around the club would huddle with a beer or pernod and water in the dark recesses of the clubroom and go on Lord Buckley's charted trips. He was a teller of allegories—a white man who spoke in the idiom and slang of black jazz musicians. His stories were full of beauty and soul and humanity. We became drunk on the visions of this dreamlike and tragic man who was called a comedian by some people in those days. Lord Buckley would come in at night, dressed in an old beautiful suit, a flower fresh in his lapel, gracious to all, with hugs, with deep laughs and strange sighs, always gentle, always uneven in the rambling levels of his midnight confrontation with demons and saints. He was vulnerable to near perfection. A quiet legend even before his time was over, he died of starvation and thoughtlessness during the attempt by the city police of New York to prevent people without cabaret cards from making a living, from working at the only thing they knew how to do. This brutality of spirit, inherent in red tape and in the affairs of the state, was the very thing he could not cope with. It is the antithesis of love. And Lord Buckley's life was full of love.

The Gate of Horn floats in my memory, a long trip down Lakeshore Drive in the Anglia after work at three in the morning and a lonely frightened late-night walk from the Cass Hotel where I stayed because it was cheap. I was listening, talking openly for the first time in my life, about my work, about my troubles, listening to everyone else do the same thing. I was forging something out of my music . . . perhaps a new sense of awareness.

After that summer in Chicago we moved to Connecticut and lived in a red house below a cow pasture, in the middle of farming country. While I ironed or baked bread or watched the Cuban missile crisis on TV I would find a melody running around and around in my head and when I stopped to listen to it I would find myself falling in love with it. Falling in love with a song is like falling in love with a person, or getting to know someone I liked from the very start. I don't really know why, because maybe it can't be pinned down; like a smile that is just right, or the hair or the eyes, I just like them and they get into my mind and stay, and I wait to find them and learn about them. The songs always worked that way with me, weedling into my mind in the middle of making the bed or cleaning the bathtub.

Peter was teaching and Clark was walking and talking and going to nursery school and I was becoming a university wife. I took my guitar to every party we went to. We lived in a house that cost a lot of money and was out in the country and not in those plastic houses most of our graduate teaching friends lived in. So I kept working, one week there, two weeks here, home for a month, gone for a week; at one time I commuted to Boston, and each night it took me two hours up and two hours back. I sang at a club called the Golden Vanity.

On those drives home from Boston, and the long train trips through Canada and the airplane rides that took me away from the farmhouse where I lived with Peter and Clark, I began to sort out the changing feelings I had about my marriage and my work. From the very first, when I started to sing in Boulder, I felt that I was being torn away from the life we had begun to have. I ventured outward slowly, keeping the bonds of my family around the musical life that was pulling me out into the world. I wanted it both ways. I wanted the long peaceful evenings when Peter would study late and I would bake sugar cookies and read poetry. I wanted the visits with my neighbor on Brown's road, when we would talk about recipes and old crafts and how to grow geraniums in the shade. My neighbors' name was Jan Scottron and she taught me to braid rugs and make wreaths of dried pine cones and nuts and fern seed and milkweed pods. We collected them in the fall, hunting and bending and gossiping together like two birds in the autumn woods. When the heavy winter snow stranded our two families on Brown's road, we shovelled the deep drifts and sat out the storms, sharing the food and the firewood. We whiled away hours in front of the hearth, as Peter and I used to do in Denver with my father, in the winter, drinking sherry and telling stories while the snow fell outside. I wanted the easy unthinking continuity of life in that place. We were beginning to be part of the university community. We had friends who taught, and had Friday night potluck dinners and bring-your-own parties and everyone was very gay.

But in the peaceful haze of it there was something crucial missing. Peter and I lived together but we didn't talk much. We didn't know how to talk. We assumed, at least for a while, that the way things were going was just a result of my working. I would leave for a week or so, and while I was gone Peter would study and take care of Clark. Clark went to nursery school in the daytime. Daddy was home at night. Sometimes when I crawled into bed in the middle of the night, after coming in from some far city, I felt we should talk, look, listen to each other. But we were too often silent.

I found myself searching for love, for friendship, for clarity outside my marriage, away from Peter, on the road. At the same time something in me wanted to return to the slow, easy days of university life. I was caught in the reality of my life away from home, a life of cheap hotels and dingy folk-music clubs. In New York I stayed at the Broadway Central Hotel and worked at Gerde's Folk City, the old hang-out of the folkmusic crowd. There were long hours, sour-smelling dressing rooms, and that last late set that must be done, even when there were only two or three people to listen. At three in the morning I would be trying to sleep, trying to make a home out of a green hotel room near the Bowery or near Rush street in Chicago, or in Denver, when I worked at the Exodus. But the real pleasure came from the music. It was the harness in which I worked. I knew my music would grow. But my marriage wasn't growing, the relationship was going nowhere. Peter blamed my career, and still does. I blame our youth perhaps. But the world beckoned, life beckoned, and I had to go on. I left Peter because we were no longer in the same place, and there was too much painful distance between us to find the way back. I told Peter that I was going to leave him at the end of the summer of 1962. We groped for each other then, and for a while tried to heal the wounds and patch up the broken promises. But nothing would suffice. I don't think we meant to hurt each other. We had grown apart.

I left the house in the country to the dying of the leaves, to the ending of summer.

When I left my husband I had just done my first Carnegie Hall concert as Theodore Bikel's guest. My parents had come all the way from Denver to see me sing at Carnegie. My mother wept at the sight of the carriages in Central Park in the late October air and my father struck up a friendship with a convict-sailor character in the village who gave him a grand tour of the smells and sounds of Greenwich village. Dad always said the guy picked *them* up, walking beside them and telling dirty stories till my father broke up laughing and accepted the invitation to visit cheese stores, vegetable markets down by the Hudson, the docks where the loads of beef come in to be hung and distributed to this big hungry island city. In the damp river air, mother hurried along beside them under the awnings and leaf-bare trees while the crazy sailor showed the crazy blind man his city. They sat in the first row at Carnegie Hall, my parents, proud and teary-eyed. And afterwards, the success dimmed with the reality of confusion for me as I took the plane alone to Tucson where I had a job for a week.

The next morning, after flying all day and singing all night, I went to the doctor to find out why my lungs had been gurgling and what the great pain in my chest was. All summer the pleurisy I had was trying to say stop . . . rest . . . think. Now, out in Tucson where the sunsets were purple and orange and every color of the rainbow on my own pale skin, I was tucked into a hospital, surrounded with the tender care of a doctor who was sympathetic and competent. The couple who ran the coffee house where I spent one exhausted night also worked as bio-chemists for Dr. Schneider and there was a little circle of friends around. Fran and Lou brought me chicken soups and chocolate bars and tacos. I was way down at the end of the adobe hall, well out of the way of patients who are leery of this frightening, little-known disease called TB. Dr. Schneider brought me books by Albert Camus, Bertrand Russell and André Gide. He said he wouldn't let me read the "Magic Mountain" just then; it was something I would have to get around to later. I felt protected from my own pain, somehow. Not physical pain, because there wasn't much of it after the liquid was out of my lungs and the pills and hypos started to make some headway. But the pain in my mind hid like a coward behind the books, the incredible sunsets that I watched from my screened-in porch, the long laughing talks with Fran and Lou and the sleeping pills that came before the long nights. Somewhere inside me there was a desert made of secrets and strength-sapping journeys, lonely Canadian bus rides and bad dreams. It lay bone dry and unable to grow even a weed or a cactus.

For a month in the adobe hospital in Tucson, I tried to learn to play the guitar properly. I got a Carcasi guitar method book and practiced all morning. When the sun was high, I went out on the screened-in porch to watch the slow changing color in the Arizona air. I read all afternoon in the cool of the room on my bed, gobbled down my dinner and giggled with the nurses or Fran and Lou and Bill Taxerman. Then I wrote some vague letters to people who all lived somewhere I had called home . . . Denver, Boulder, Chicago, Storrs, Connecticut. I was out there like a kite, hanging on the thread of voices over the telephone and letters that came at lunchtime. I never learned to play the guitar right, but the desert inside my heart started slowly to open up to the sun and rain, slowly budded and began to bloom again.

After spending a month in the hospital in Tucson, I was admitted to National Jewish Hospital in Denver where I spent four months (1962-63). My room looked like a studio. I had a tape recorder and a guitar, and a typewriter, and a record player. My roommate was from Viet-Nam, a beautiful delicate girl whose name in English means Snow-flower. She taught me how to knit and make bean curd soup. And she was kind to me in the moments when I was torn with guilt and confusion about leaving Peter. Clark was with me, staying with my mother, until Peter came and took him to Connecticut on the advise of his lawyer. Already, the divorce was being put through, and the city of New York was the only place I felt I could go now. The music pulled me, the music that was being written and sung; the poet-singers who hung out in the village and listened to Dylan rap or sing at Gerde's where the noise at the bar quieted only once in a while and mostly for him; where people still drank wine and hung out around Bleecker Street. There the focus of city music found its way, straggling in from Minnesota with Bob Dylan, from the Western American Indian with Peter La Farge and Buffy St. Marie, from Brooklyn with Jack Elliott who turned western and to this day behaves more like a cowhand riding fences on a wind-blown south forty than a New York native son. They were all part of that lure, the city, the village.

When they let me out of the hospital room and told me my chest x-ray was clear and gave me a hundred bottles of pills to take for another 18 months, I went straight to New York.

The coming of the roads

With quiet melancholy

Words and Music by Billy Edd Wheeler

1. Now that our moun-tain is grow - - ing with peo-ple hun-gry for wealth, How come, it's you that's a-go - - ing, and

I'm left a - lone by my - self?

We used to hunt the cool cav - - erns

deep in our for - est of green.

Then came the road and the tav - - erns, and

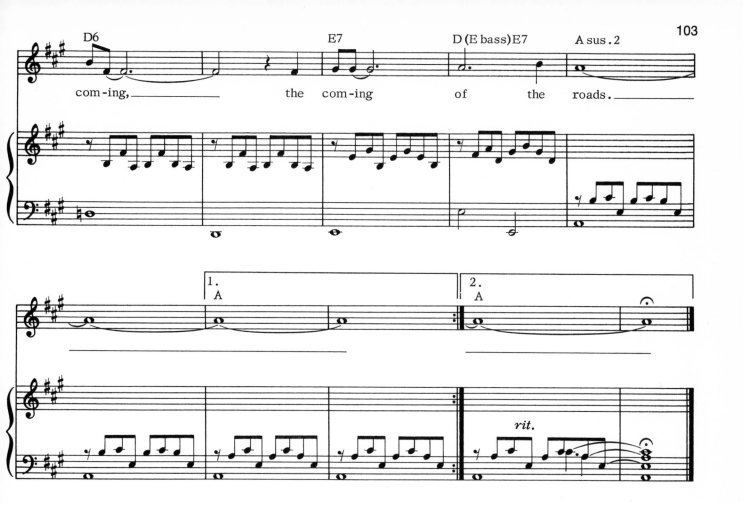

com-ing, _____ the com-ing of the roads. _____

2. Look how they've cut all to pieces
   Our ancient poplar and oak.
   And the hillsides are stained with the greases
   That burned up the heavens with smoke.
   You used to curse the bold crewmen
   Who stripped our earth of its ore.
   Now you've changed, and you've gone over to them
   And you've learned to love what you hated before.
   Once I thanked God for my treasure,
   Now like rust, it corrodes,
   And I can't help from blaming your going
   On the coming,
   On the coming of the roads.

I slept in the attic of Bob's house in Woodstock one night in 1965.
From the little stone-walled writing room at three in the morning I heard this
whole song for the first time, with the moon full and the house still
except for his singing and guitar.

mr. tambourine man

Words and Music by Bob Dylan

Moderately

Hey, Mis - ter Tam - bou - rine Man, play a song for me,— I'm not sleep-y and— there ain't no place I'm go - ing to.— Hey, Mis - ter Tam-

D.S. al Fine

2. Take me on a trip upon your magic swirlin' ship,
   My senses have been stripped,
   My hands can't feel to grip,
   My toes too numb to step,
   Wait only for my boot heels to be wanderin'.
   I'm ready to go anywhere,
   I'm ready for to fade
   Into my own parade.
   Cast your dancin' spell my way,
   I promise to go under it.
   Chorus

3. Though you might hear laughin', spinnin', swingin' madly through the sun,
   It's not aimed at anyone,
   It's just escapin' on the run,
   And but for the sky there are no fences facin'.
   And if you hear vague traces
   Of skippin' reels of rhyme
   To your tambourine in time,
   It's just a ragged clown behind,
   I wouldn't pay it any mind,
   It's just a shadow
   You're seein' that he's chasin'.
   Chorus

4. Take me disappearin' through the smoke rings of my mind
   Down the foggy ruins of time,
   Far past the frozen leaves,
   The haunted, frightened trees
   Out to the windy beach
   Far from the twisted reach of crazy sorrow.
   Yes, to dance beneath the diamond sky
   With one hand wavin' free,
   Silhouetted by the sea,
   Circled by the circus sands,
   With memory and fate
   Driven deep beneath the waves.
   Let me forget about today until tomorrow.
   Chorus

So Early In The Spring

With motion

Adapted by Mary Robbins

1. So ear - ly,

ear - - ly_ in the spring, I shipped on board_____ to serve my

king, I left my dear - - est_ dear be -

2. My love she takes me by the hand.
   "If ever I marry you'll be the man."
   A thousand vows, so long and sweet,
   Saying, "We'll be married when next we meet."

3. And all the time I sailed the seas,
   I could not find a moment's ease,
   In thinking of my dearest dear,
   And never a word from her could I hear.

4. At last we sailed into Glasgow-town.
   I strode the streets both up and down,
   Inquiring of my dearest dear,
   And never a word from her could I hear.

5. I went straightway to her Father's Hall,
   And loudly for my love did call.
   "My daughter's married, she's a rich man's wife,
   She's married to another much better for life."

6. If the girl is married that I adore,
   I'm sure I'll stay on land no more.
   I'll sail the sea till the day I die.
   I'll break the waves rolling mountain high.

*Love without possession, or a fantasy of freedom,
or a deja-vu caught from the window of an east-bound train—all,
and more.*

DADDY, YOU'VE BEEN ON MY MIND

Words and Music by Bob Dylan

1. Per - haps it's the col - or of the sun cut

flat An' cov - er - in' _____ the cross-roads I'm

2. I don't mean trouble, please don't put me down or get upset,
   I am not pleadin' or sayin', "I can't forget,"
   I do not walk the floor bowed down an' bent, but yet,
   Daddy, you're just on my mind.

3. Even though my mind is hazy an' my thoughts they might be narrow,
   Where you been don't bother me nor bring me down in sorrow,
   It don't even matter to me where you're wakin' up tomorrow,
   Daddy, you're just on my mind.

4. I am not askin' you to say words like "yes" and "no,"
   Please understand me, I got no place for you t' go,
   I'm just breathin' to myself pretendin' not that I don't know,
   Daddy, you been on my mind.

5. When you wake up in the mornin', baby, look inside your mirror,
   You know I won't be next to you, you know I won't be near,
   I'd just be curious to know if you can see yourself as clear
   As someone who has had you on her mind.

When we recorded this song in 1965 in New York,
Dick played the dulcimer and Mimi sat beautiful and smiling in the booth,
and their big German Shepherd, Lush, romped through the studio,
barking and guarding us all.

Pack Up Your Sorrows

Words and Music by Richard Fariña and Pauline Marden

No use cry - ing, talk - ing to a stran - ger

Nam - ing the sor - rows you've seen, ___

Too man-y sad times, ___ too man-y bad ___ times,

all to me. me.

Interlude

D. S.

2. No use rambling, walking in the shadows,
   Trailing a wandering star.
   No one beside you, no one to hide you,
   And nobody knows where you are.
   Chorus

3. No use gambling, running in the darkness,
   Looking for a spirit that's free.
   Too many wrong times, too many long times,
   Nobody knows what you see.
   Chorus

4. No use roaming, lying by the roadside,
   Seeking a satisfied mind.
   Too many highways, too many byways,
   And nobody's walking behind.
   Chorus

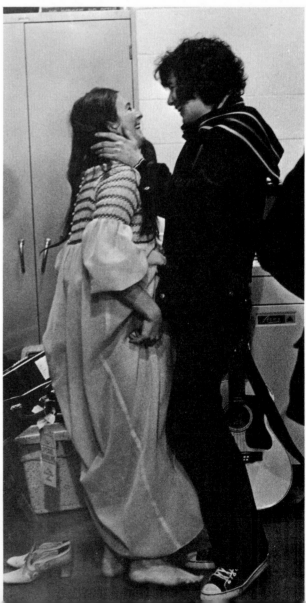

Christmas time, 1964, Harry Tufts had a party in his beautiful folklore center in Denver, among guitars and pine boughs. For one of his gentle gifts he made me a present of this song.

LORD GREGORY

Adapted by Mary Robbins

1. I am the queen's daugh-ter, I come from Câ-pa - kin In

search of Lord Greg-o-ry, Pray God I find him.

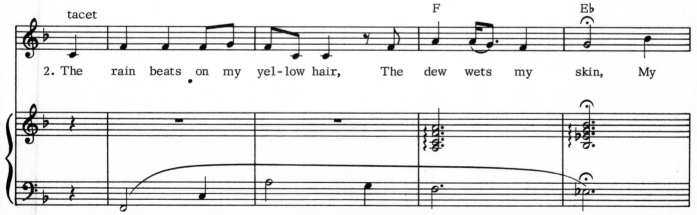

2. The rain beats on my yel-low hair, The dew wets my skin, My

wee babe's cold in my arms, Lord Greg - o - ry, let me in. 3. Lord

Greg - o - ry, he ___ is not here, I swear, can't ___ be seen, He's

gone to bon - nie Scot - land for to bring home a fair queen.

D.C.

4. So leave now these portals,
   And likewise this hall,
   For it's deep in the sea
   You should hide your downfall.

5. Oh, don't you remember, love,
   That night at Câpa-kin
   When we exchanged rings, love,
   And I against my will?

6. Yours was pure silver,
   And mine was but tin.
   Yours cost a guinea,
   And mine but a pin.

7. My curse on you, Mother.
   My curse being so,
   I dreamed that my true love
   Came a-knockin' at my door.

8. Lie down now, my foolish son,
   Lie down now and sleep.
   'Twas only the servant girl
   Lies drowned in the deep.

9. Go saddle my black horse,
   The brown or the bay!
   Go saddle my fastest horse
   In the stable this day.

10. I'll ride over mountains
    And valleys so wide.
    I'll find the girl that I love
    And lie by her side.

THirSTY BOOTS

Words and Music by Eric Andersen

1. You've long been on the o-pen road,_ You've been sleep-ing in_ the rain. From dirt - y words and

mud-dy cells_ your clothes are smeared and stained._ But the

dirt - y words, the mud-dy cells_ Will soon be judged in

shame; So on - ly stop_ to rest your-self And

you'll be off a - gain._____ Then

124

look-ing for___ the eve - ning,___ for the

morn - ing in___ your eye.

2. Then

2. Then tell me of the ones you've seen as far as you could see,
Across the plain from field to town a-marching to be free,
And of the rusted prison gates that tumbled by degree,
Like laughing children one by one they looked like you and me.
Chorus

3. I know you are no stranger down the crooked rainbow trails,
From dancing cliff-edged shattered sills of slandered-shackled jails,
But the melodies drift from below as the walls are being scaled.
Yes, all of this and more, my friend, your song shall not be failed.
Chorus twice

Gordon still sings this song better than anyone can.
It grabs you like the roar of an airplane engine, or a train whistle a long way off.

early mornin' rain

Words and Music by Gordon Lightfoot

In the ear-ly morn-in' rain_____ With a dol-lar in my

hand, With an ach-in' in my heart_____

And my pock-ets full of sand, I'm a long way from

2. Out on runway number nine
   Big seven-o-seven set to go,
   Well, I'm stuck here on the grass,
   Where the cold wind blows.
   Well, the liquor tasted good,
   And the time went fast.
   Well, there she goes, my friend,
   There she's rollin' now at last.

3. Hear the mighty engines roar,
   See the silver bird on high,
   She's away and westward bound
   Far above the clouds she'll fly,
   Where the mornin' rain don't fall
   And the sun always shines.
   She'll be flyin' o'er my home
   In about three hours time.

4. Well, this old airport's got me down,
   It ain't no earthly good to me,
   'Cause I'm stuck here on the ground
   As cold and drunk as I can be.
   You can't jump a jet plane
   Like you can a freight train,
   So I best be on my way
   In the early mornin' rain.

*The way I sang this song with Dick Fariña playing the dulcimer
is the way I live it . . . or singing it at Big Sur with
Gil Turner . . . or just by myself driving somewhere, singing soft.*

carry it on

Words & Music by Gil Turner

With deep feeling, gospel style

1. There's a
2. They will

man _____ by my side a - walk - in', _____ There's a
tell _____ their ly - in' sto - ries, _____ Send _ their

3. Oh, their dogs will lie there rottin',
   All their lies will be forgotten,
   All their prison walls will crumble,
   Carry it on, carry it on,
   Carry it on, carry it on.

4. If you can't go on any longer,
   Take the hand held by your brother.
   Ev'ry victory goin' to bring another.
   Carry it on, carry it on,
   Carry it on, carry it on.

5. There's a man by my side walkin',
   There's a voice within me talkin',
   It's a word that needs a-sayin',
   Carry it on, carry it on,
   Carry it on, carry it on.

I hope when I am as old as Malvina
is I am as young as she has been all her life.

IT ISN'T NICE

Words by Malvina Reynolds
Music by Malvina Reynolds & Barbara Dane

Rock-'n-roll style

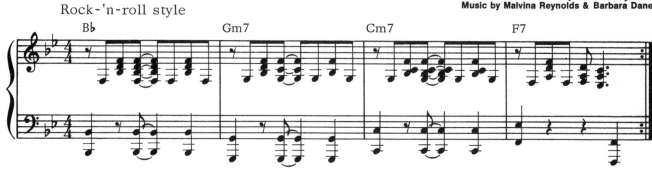

It is-n't nice to block the door - way, It is-n't nice to

go to jail,____ There are nic - er ways to do it,

2. It isn't nice to dump the groceries,
   Or to sleep in on the floor,
   Or to shout our cry of freedom
   In the hotel or the store,
   It isn't nice, it isn't nice,
   You told us once, you told us twice,
   But if that's freedom's price,
   We don't mind . . .

3. Yeah, we tried negotiations
   And the token picket line,
   Mister Charlie didn't see us
   And he might as well be blind;
   When you deal with men of ice,
   You can't deal with ways so nice,
   But if that's freedom's price,
   We don't mind . . .

4. They kidnapped boys in Mississippi,
   They shot Medgar in the back,
   Did you say that wasn't proper?
   Did you stand out on the track?
   You were quiet just like mice,
   Now you say we're not nice,
   Well, if that's freedom's price,
   We don't mind . . .

5. It isn't nice to block the doorways,
   It isn't nice to go to jail,
   There are nicer ways to do it,
   But the nice ways always fail,
   It isn't nice, it isn't nice,
   You told us once, you told us twice,
   Thanks, buddy, for your advice,
   Well, if that's freedom's price,
        We don't mind . . .
        WE DON'T MIND!

PART 5

We will never show people who we
are until we know who we are; we
will never go anywhere until we
know where we are.
Malcolm X

Notes from Mississippi
Sunday, August 1, 1964
We arrived in Jackson on the plane at 5:00 in the afternoon, after flying
in from Newark airport. There was a purple and deep red sunset that nearly
covered the sky of Jackson like a cloak of blood; the light of the sun passed
through it to the wet pavements and the thick green grass. The humidity
was high and walking was a little like swimming. Bob and Sue Cohen
picked us up at the airport. We drove to the COFO office. Driving along,
Bob began to talk about what was going on. He started with the basic
rules about traveling, (never travel integrated, for instance,) no mingling
with Negroes in most public spots, with the exception of one or two places
in Jackson that are integrated restaurants. All the instructions given in the
legal guide were restated. Barbara Dane was with me. Those first couple
of days in Jackson were made really easier by her being there with me.

The office of COFO in the city is located in a Negro neighborhood on
Lynch street. I first saw the address and thought someone was being
funny. But there it is, and I had my first feeling of the security I was going
to learn to feel when I reached a Negro neighborhood. The most frightening
thing of all was to be in a white neighborhood in Mississippi. Communist
is probably the most widely used term for the whites and Negroes that are
working in the movement. It is a catch-phrase in this country, anyway, for
anyone who doesn't hold the view that America is all-good and all-pure.
There is that particular feeling in Mississippi that these "outside agitators"
are directed by Communist front people. It seems to give them an excuse to
do anything they please to the people in the movement.

Barbara and I stayed at a motel that first night in Jackson, a place called
Sun and Sand, of all things. Almost as ludicrous as Lynch street; it was
only recently integrated. Out of about 300 rooms in the motel, 197 of
them were taken by people who were working in various capacities in the
movements. There were doctors who had come down for two or three
weeks, and lawyers who came to defend the people who get arrested and
put in jail on trumped-up charges. I felt very strange staying there, with
the big pool and the room-service, on my first night in Jackson. I would
have preferred to be in the office, using the sleeping bag I brought. But
there were so many people in the city that there was just no room for us
to stay except there. So Barbara and I had a swim and listened to the long
southern drawls of the people who were guests. We wondered at their
ability to dance to the rock-and-roll music that they played, and at the same

time refuse simple human rights to the people who were, and still are the basis of that music. They dig it, and think it's theirs, not looking at where it came from, really, nor caring.

I felt afraid of all the people who were white and not connected with the movement, who were at the motel.

We got to Greenville after a trip through the lovely countryside of northeast Mississippi. Every pickup truck we see carries a double gun rack in the back window. We drive under the speed limit and it is extremely hot. It is like going on outpost expeditions in a war. The difference is that we carry no weapon. Only the enemy is armed, and he has everything from Thompson's tank in Jackson to people loaded with hate and guns in all the other parts of the state.

When the 2000-year-old man was asked what mode of transportation was most frequent in the old days, he replied . . . "Fear" . . . It must still be true. I had never lived before with actual, tangible fear in my life, on a constant level.

Monday
Greenville is very quiet. The progress in registration seems to be at a standstill. People are just not interested enough in what is going on to really care about getting the vote, or joining the Freedom Democratic Party. There is hardly any "security" in Greenville. We walk about freely, integrated, going to cafes and even drinking beer in the Freedom House. Charles Cox is the head of the COFO office there. He is from Howard University and will probably go back to school this fall after having been here in the state for two years. He inspires a feeling of great confidence. There is a minister here from one of the Southern colleges. He must be about 60; he and his wife are here with the Council of Churches volunteer force. He seems a good man, too, and his wife is motherly and white-haired and very patient.

Returning at 5:30 to the office, we were told we were going to Drew, a nearby town, to sing at a voter registration meeting. (In Sunflower country, 68 percent of the population is Negro. Out of 25,000 eligible voters, less than 200 are registered to vote.)

We were told that Drew is a dangerous place to go. We were told that we should expect to go to jail. The police had said that after the COFO workers accused them of harassing, and not protecting, they were prepared to look on at whatever might happen to the people who went there—that they would not even attempt to protect us. The girls who work for COFO in the Ruleville office were not allowed to go with us. It is a policy there that the men go, when there is an actual threat of danger. But we were the singers, there to make music at the meetings, and we piled into the truck. I expected be shot at or killed or beaten. We sang in the bus on the way . . . . . . "ain't gonna let nobody turn me 'round." It is something to know that there is nobody who can turn you around except yourself, and the singing, the music, is what makes a lot of this conviction possible.

I sat in the bus and changed the strings on my guitar to keep my hands from trembling. Their trembling made the task longer than it normally takes. Mrs. Hamer came out pretty soon and got in the car in front of us. We followed the car out of Ruleville and into Drew. I found that the only way to settle the terror inside me was to sing.

We drove into Drew and into the Negro neighborhood. It is a pretty, tree-filled, dirt-road town. Strange that it should house such hatred. The home where the meeting was held was owned by a woman whose son was beaten nearly to death only a few months ago by the sheriff who sat outside the house, in his car, during the whole of our meeting. Mrs. Hamer spoke to us; she who had been beaten and arrested and harassed for saying that she has a right to vote, to vote, man. She was fired from her job the day after she registered in 1962 in Sunflower county, Indianolla, the lady of dignity who stood up and sang with us. "This little light of mine . . ." She led us in singing that song, and the police cars roamed the area and the cars of the Klan circled the block and the town stood in horror at the gall of 75 Negroes who had come to sing about freedom and listen to a beautiful woman talk about the right of a man to be human.

I remember how you sang a song to put yourself to sleep,
The melody I knew you knew you never would repeat.
The candles in the silver dark were lighting up the air,
The songs I don't remember now were fingers in my hair.

I tried to hold and tell you that I knew the songs were mine
You brought them back from far away and in the night they shine
But where I heard them now I can't remember. It is clear
My ears are clogged with childhood and my face is full of fear.

After the summer of 1964, I remember most things in a kind of vague pattern. I had lost the custody of my son Clark at the end of the summer. After the court made the decision and the papers were final, I was told that one of the strongest objections they had to giving me custody, besides the fact that I lived in another state, was my being in psychotherapy. I was stunned. Rockland County court in Connecticut then, was also the enemy of my growth as a woman. They felt I did not deserve to grow and to have my son at the same time.

Life went on, straggling in a procession of concerts and airplane rides and long and short love affairs. A week after I found out that I could not legally have my son with me, I had a concert in Grand Junction, Colorado. I left my big lonely apartment at six in the morning, headed for the airport and flew to Denver, changed planes at about two o'clock and picked up the puddle-jumper that serves the mountains. We bounded over Aspen and Gunnison and arrived in the late afternoon. The land there is vast, cut with the red earth strip that makes the Garden of the Gods further south and Red Rocks Amphitheater outside of Denver.

A lean young man dressed in an uncomfortable looking suit, very proper and shy, came to meet me at the airport. He drove me, with his girl friend who was shyer than he, to the motel. After I checked in, they offered to take me to see the campus. I can hear his words again, the tall Colorado boy, as I remember back to the day, words telling me: ". . . here is the theater where you will sing . . . here is the cafeteria where we eat, would you like dinner?—We are a two-year college . . . most of the kids aren't much into politics . . . this is our beautiful subterranean bookstore and giftshop, isn't it great? . . . We are proud of it . . . we are so glad you could come all the way out here to sing . . . are you on a tour, are you on a tour, are you . . .?"

I stood in front of the window of the downstairs bookstore, looking through the huge sheet of plate glass, seeing the covers arranged, spread out, faces, words, colors, all bunched together, and strewn about at the same time, books on everything that could possibly be important or interesting or necessary for a young college student, all in words, printed in books whose pages, if you turned them, would fold and fold and turn and turn and answer anything, anything. I have tried to understand what happened to my mind at that moment. Something snapped, sprung, went out of line. It was as if one frame of a movie had spilled out of the projector and rolled endlessly onto the floor, piling the film into a winding mass, incomprehensible, impossible to untie. It was as if the film of one frame were shown over and over and over on the screen, never a change, never a respite. My hands were shaking and my breath was fast; my palms were wet and I felt as if I would fall into, onto, through, beyond the plate glass window, on the books and faces and words where I would disappear. I felt at the same time that I was losing control, going mad, and fading away from everything that was happening around me.

I turned to the boy who stood quiet and shy, so hoping I would like his campus, his girl, his soft dark blue suit, his funny smile that showed the crevices where the sun had gotten soaked up off the Colorado landscape and into his talk and his walk and his ways, and I said, "Please take me back to the hotel, I am sick."

He was sorry, he said, and we walked across the flat lawn to the car and I got in and said nothing. We drove through the broad center of town with its one-story bars and grocery stores and wide western streets. It was about four in the afternoon by then and clumps of students were heading along the streets toward dormitories with loads of books in their arms and short-sleeved shirts sticking to the smalls of their backs from the afternoon heat. They looked to me as if they were all swimming, turning and moving slowly as we drove by. The signs for the concert were curled around the telephone poles and leaned up against the inside windows of the restaurants and gas stations. I got out at the motel and thanked the boy who said he hoped I felt better, and that he would be over to pick me up about seven for the concert.

I lay on the bed for a long time with no thoughts in my mind, only the sheer physical awareness of fear. No outlet, no letup, just weighted heavily in my body like a drug injected from an endless tube that hung in coils around the room and originated somewhere states or years away, in the thoughtless past . . . Finally, I reached the decision I knew I had to reach. I must go home; now. I had to leave, this very afternoon. I had to get back to New York. I had to get connected to something I could touch, could feel; I was hanging out in space again, without getting home I would never find the thread that led back.

I called Harold Leventhal, my manager, at the office, way back in New York, where somehow my only connection with sanity seemed to be. Harold is the most honest and kindest and funniest man I know. He had managed me then for about a year, maybe two. He started managing the Weavers twenty years ago; they needed someone to put their lives together and arrange things, so he left the family business to his brother-in-law. There are only a few people in the whole business who have the kind of reputation he has. He has conscience, and concern for the things that are more intangible than money. Pete Seeger, Ronny Gilbert, Alan Arkin, Woody and Arlo Guthrie, Cisco Houston, Theo Bikel, Tom Paxton for a while, all the people he works with are committed to the things they believe in. I think I would trust Harold with anything. That afternoon was the first time I realized just how aware he is. He knew exactly what the problem was, and I had forgotten it in the midst of my panic. He said, "If you want to come home, you must come home." Never a pressure, never a hesitation in his voice. I needed help, and there he was.

I called my analyst; I had a drink to see if it would help. I found out what the plane schedule was. There was one plane out of Grand Junction to Denver and it left at seven that night. I took a bath and had another drink and packed my guitar and my suitcase. When the young man came to take me to the concert I said, "I'm terribly sorry, I am going to go home. Please take me to the airport."

I hope you read this, Colorado boy, and come to understand. You didn't say anything either, didn't try to change my mind or pry into the reasons. You walked to the car and drove me to the airport and waved goodbye. I don't know your name, but it doesn't matter. You were beautiful.

So the slow, groping, process of growing up had a push, a shove. But I was so unaware of what I was going through that for months afterwards I had to ask my friends, Harold, my doctor, what was it that had happened the week before I went to Grand Junction? I didn't want to accept the fact of my loss of Clark. It finally began to sink into my thick skull that I was not a liberated woman yet, at the heart of everything, able to be rational about it all. I was irrational and close to hysteria because my child was not with me, couldn't be with me according to the court, and I was first of all, in my guts, a mother. I would not kidnap Clark back or haggle over him or pull him apart like a piece of property or scream at his father that he should be with me, he was my baby. The battle, bitter and enraged, was waging itself with a force greater than I could handle, inside my heart. This torment went on for four more years, while I visited Clark everytime I could. I wrote letters, made phone calls and spent summers and Christmases with my son and tried not to burden strangers with my pain or think too much about it when I was alone. My music carried me, buoyed me up in a sea of anger and unhappiness.

At the end of 1967 Clark told his father that he wanted to come and live with me, and has been with me ever since. I am a mother again. I am more a complete woman than I could have been without him. And my music doesn't come and go with elation or sorrow; it is always there, faithful in its way, as an old lover or an over-night guest. It can take care of itself, with a little help from its friends.

To Leonard, with love:
singing Suzanne gets me higher than anything.

suzanne

Words and Music by Leonard Cohen

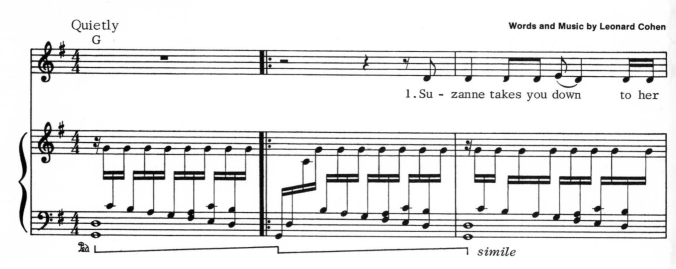

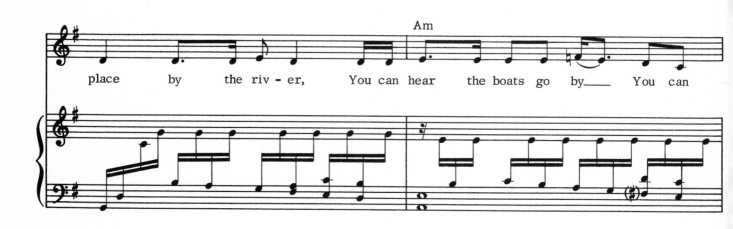

want to trav - el with her, and you want to trav - el blind,___ And you

know that you can trust her, For you've touched her per - fect bod - y with your

1. - 2.

3.

mind.

mind._____

2. And Jesus was a sailor
   When He walked upon the water,
   And He spent a long time watching
   From a lonely wooden tower,
   And when He knew for certain
   Only drowning men could see Him
   He said, "All men shall be brothers, then,
   Until the sea shall free them,"
   But He Himself was broken
   Long before the sky would open,
   Forsaken, almost human,
   He sank beneath your wisdom
   Like a stone.

   Chorus:
   And you want to travel with Him,
   And you want to travel blind,
   And you think you maybe trust Him,
   For He's touched your perfect body,
   With His mind.

3. Suzanne takes you down
   To her place by the river,
   You can hear the boats go by,
   You can spend the night forever,
   And the sun pours down like honey
   On our lady of the harbour;
   And she shows you where to look
   Amid the garbage and the flowers.
   There are heroes in the seaweed,
   There are children in the morning,
   They are leaning out for love,
   And they will lean that way forever,
   While Suzanne holds the mirror.

   Chorus:
   And you want to travel with her,
   And you want to travel blind,
   And you think maybe you'll trust her,
   For you've touched her perfect body,
   With your mind.

La Colombe

English Lyric by Alasdair Clayre
Music and French lyric by Jacques Brel

Moderato, but with intensity

1. Why all these bu-gles cry-ing   For squads of young men drilled   To kill and____ to be killed,   And wait-ing by this train.   Why the or-ders

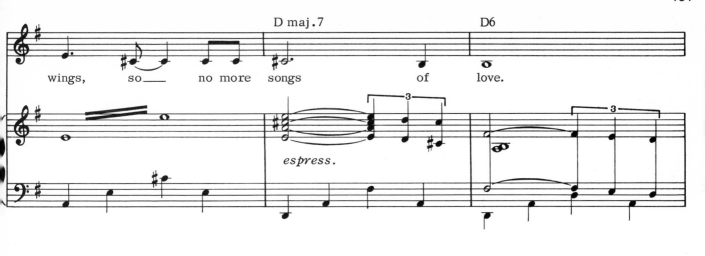

wings, so___ no more songs of love.

espress.

We are not here to sing, We're here___ to kill the dove.

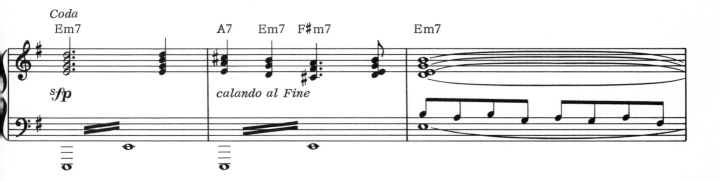

calando al Fine

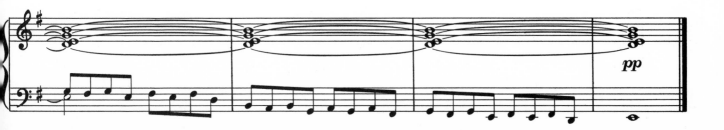

1. Why all these bugles crying
   For squads of young men drilled
   To kill and to be killed,
   And waiting by this train.

   Why the orders loud and hoarse,
   Why the engine's groaning cough
   As it strains to drag us off
   Into the holocaust.

   Why crowds who sing and cry
   And shout and fling us flowers,
   And trade their right for ours
   To murder and to die?

   Refrain:
   The dove has torn her wings,
     so no more songs of love.
   We are not here to sing,
     we're here to kill the dove.

2. Why has this moment come
   When childhood has to die,
   When hope shrinks to a sigh
   And speech into a drum.

   Why are they pale and still,
   Young boys trained overnight,
   Conscripts forced to fight
   And dressed in grey to kill.

   These rain clouds massing tight,
   This trainload battle bound,
   This moving burial ground
   Sent thund'ring toward the night?
   Refrain

1. Pourquoi cette fanfare
   Quand les soldats par quatre
   Attendent les massacres
   Sur le quai d'une gare.

   Pourquoi ce train ventru
   Qui ronronne et soupire
   Avant de nous conduire
   Jusqu'au malentendu.

   Pourquoi les chants les cris
   Des foules venues fleurir
   Ceux qui ont le droit de partir
   Au nom de leurs conneries.

   Refrain:
   Nous n'irons plus au bois
     la colombe est blessée.
   Nous n'allons pas au bois,
     nous allons la tuer.

2. Pourquoi l'heure que voilà
   Où finit notre enfance,
   Où finit notre chance,
   Où notre train s'en va.

   Pourquoi ce lourd convoi
   Chargé d'hommes en gris,
   Repeints en une nuit
   Pour partir en soldats.

   Pourquoi ce train de pluie,
   Pourquoi ce train de guerre,
   Pourquoi ce cimetière
   En marche vers la nuit?
   Refrain

3. Why statues tow'ring brave
   Above the last defeat,
   Old words and lies repeat
   Across the new made grave.

   Why the same still-birth
   That vict'ry always brought,
   These hours of glory bought
   By men with mouths of earth.

   Dead ash without a spark,
   Where cities glittered bright
   For guns probe ev'ry light
   And crush it in the dark.
   Refrain

4. And why your face undone
   With jagged lines of tears
   That gave in those first years
   All peace I ever won.

   Your body in the gloom,
   The platform fading back
   Your shadow on the track
   A flower on a tomb.

   And why these days ahead,
   When I must let you cry
   And live prepared to die,
   As if our love were dead.
   Refrain

I love this song—but Michael Sahl,
electronic composer and my pianist in 1968–9, loves it even more.

Hard Loving Loser

Words and Music by Richard Fariña

Fast, with drive

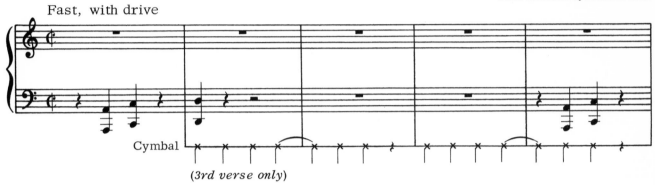

Cymbal

(3rd verse only)

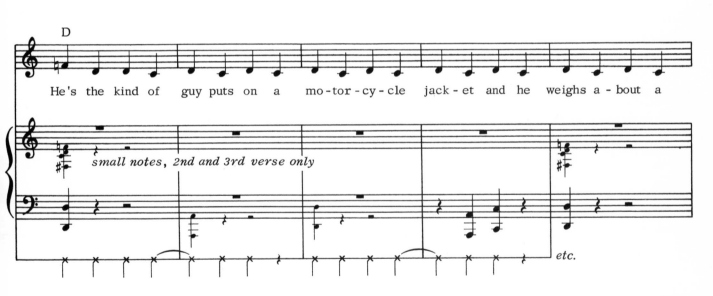

D

He's the kind of guy puts on a mo-tor-cy-cle jack-et and he weighs a-bout a

small notes, 2nd and 3rd verse only

etc.

hun-dred and five____   He's the kind of surf-er got a ho-dad-dy hair-

frost's on the pump - kin and the lit - tle girls are jump - in' he's a hard lov - in' son - of - a - gun,___ He's got 'em wait - ing down - stairs just to sam - ple his af - fairs___ and they call him a spoon - ful of fun.___

2. He's the kind of person going riding on a skate board
    and his mind's ragin' out of control.
He's the kind of person goes to drive a Maserati
    puts the key inside the wrong little hole.
He's the kind of ski-bum tearing wild down the mountain
    hits a patch where there ain't any snow.
He's the kind of cowboy got a hot trigger finger,
    shoots his boot, 'cause he's drawing kind of slow.
But when he comes in for bowling, he's an expert at rolling,
    sets the pins up and lays them right down.
He's got them taking off their heels,
    and they like the way he feels,
And they call him a carnival clown.

3. Well, he's got a parachute and screaming like Geronimo
    and makes a little hole in the ground.
He's the kind of logger when the man hollers timber,
    has to stop and look around for the sound.
He's the kind of artist rents a groovy little attic
    and discovers that he can't grow a beard.
He's a human cannonball, come in for a landing
    and he wonders where the net disappeared.
But when he takes off his shoes, it won't come as news,
    that they're lining up in threes and in twos.
He's got them pounding on the door,
    got them begging for some more,
And they call him whatever they choose.

There is nothing to be afraid of . . . The ultimate reassurance and the ultimate terror.
The Politics of Experience—R. D. Laing

Dress Rehearsal Rag

Words and Music by Leonard Cohen

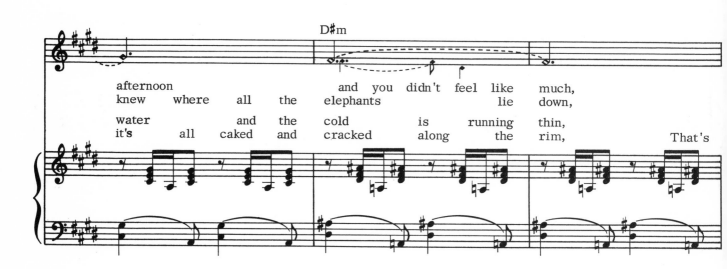

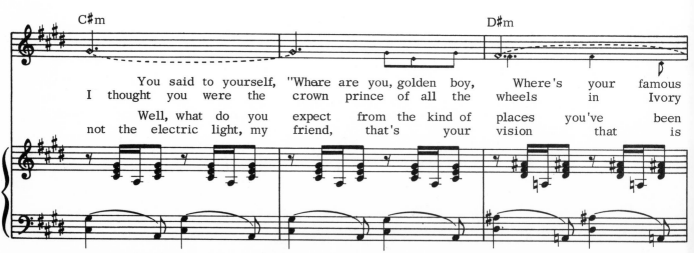

C#m

gold-en touch? 1.{ Look at your body, now, For
Town;   And a bitter voice in the mirror says, "Hey

living in? 2.{ Cover up your face with soap, there,
dim.   and you got an A for anyone who will

Bm7

there's nothing much to save,
Prince, you need a shave."
Why don't you try un-

now you're Santa Claus,
give you his ap - plause.
I thought you were a
That's a funeral in the

_sf_

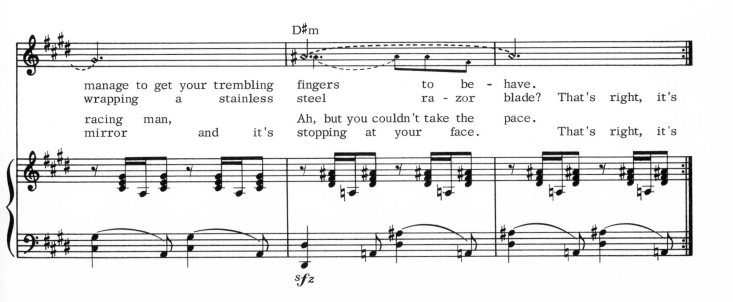

D#m

manage to get your trembling fingers to be - have.
wrapping a stainless steel ra - zor blade? That's right, it's

racing man, Ah, but you couldn't take the pace. That's right, it's
mirror and it's stopping at your face. That's right, it's

sfz

I THINK IT'S GOING TO RAIN TODAY

Words and Music by Randy Newman

Lone - ly, lone - ly,

Tin can at my feet, Think I'll kick it down the street,

That's the way to treat a friend.

Chorus:
Lonely,
Lonely,
Tin can at my feet,
Think I'll kick it down the street,
That's the way to treat a friend.

3. Bright before me the signs implore me,
   "Help the needy and show them the way."
   Human kindness overflowing
   And I think it's going to rain today.

The Littlewoods lottery sometimes makes a man rich overnight in Liverpool: more often he's a pound poorer—but still he plays.

LIVErPOOL LULLaBY

Words and Music by Stan Kelly

Oh you are a muck-y kid, Dirt-y as a dust-bin lid; When he finds out the things you did, You'll get a belt from your dad. Ah, you have your fa-ther's nose, So

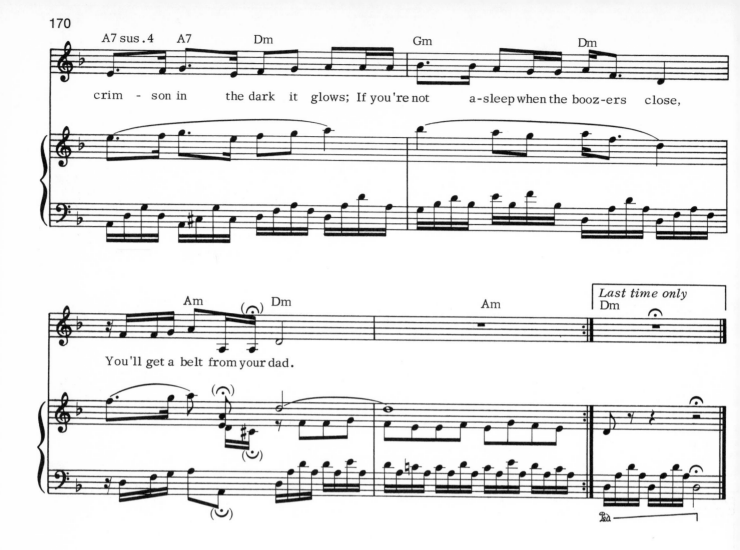

crim - son in   the dark it glows; If you're not   a-sleep when the booz-ers   close,

You'll get a belt from your dad.

Last time only

2. You look so scruffy lying there,
    Strawberry jam tufts in you hair,
    And in the world you haven't a care
        And I have got so many.
    It's quite a struggle ev'ry day
    Living on your father's pay,
    The bugger drinks it all away
        Leaves me without any.

3. Although we have no silver spoon,
    Better days are coming soon
    Now Nelly's working at the loom
        And she gets paid on Friday.
    Perhaps one day we'll have a bash
    When Littlewoods provides the cash,
    We'll get a house in Knotting Ash
        And buy your dad a brewery.

4. Oh, you are a mucky kid,
    Dirty as a dustbin lid,
    When he finds out the things you did
        You'll get a belt from your dad.
    Oh, you have your father's face,
    You're growing up a real hard case,
    But there's no one else can take your place,
        Go fast asleep for Mammy.

marat/sade

Music by Richard Peaslee
Original German Language Version of play and text by Peter Weiss
English version by Geoffrey Skelton
Verse adaptation and lyrics by Adrian Mitchell

HOMAGE TO MARAT (Part I)

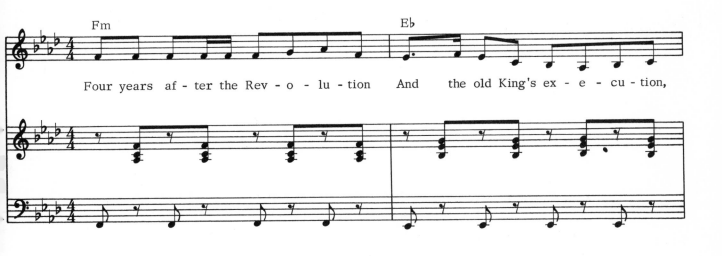

Four years af - ter the Rev - o - lu - tion And the old King's ex - e - cu - tion,

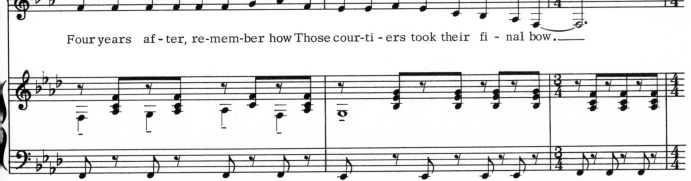

Four years af - ter, re-mem-ber how Those cour-ti - ers took their fi - nal bow._____

THE PEOPLE'S REACTION

Throw all the gen-er-als___ out on their ass.___

Why do they have the gold,

Why do they have the pow-er, Why, why, why, why, why___

___ do they have the friend at the top,___ Why do they have the jobs at the

top? We've got noth-ing, al-ways had noth-ing, Noth-ing but holes and

mil - lions of___ them, Liv-ing in holes, dy-.ing in holes,

Holes in our bel-lies and holes in our clothes.

MARAT, WE'RE POOR

Largamente

Ma-rat, we're poor and the poor stay poor, Ma-rat, don't

make us wait an-y-more. We want our rights and we don't care

how, We want— our rev-o-lu-tion Now!

8va bassa

HOMAGE TO MARAT (*Part I*)
Un poco più mosso

Four years he fought and he fought un-a-fraid,

pp   *sempre staccato*

Sniff-ing down trai-tors, by trai-tors be-trayed, Ma-rat in the court-room,

stormed through the wall of the pris-on they told us would out-last us all.

MARAT, WE'RE POOR (*reprise*)

Ma - rat, we're poor and the poor stay poor, Ma - rat, don't

make us wait an - y more. We want our rights and we don't care

how. We want our rev-o-lu-tion Now!

POOR OLD MARAT

Bm   F#m   D   Em A   D   G   A

eyes turn as red_____ as rust._____ Poor old Ma-rat, we trust in

Poco meno mosso

Bb tacet - - - - - - - p - - - - - - G

you.   Ma - rat, we're   poor_____ and the poor stay

Dm   G   Dm   F

poor,_____ Ma-rat, don't make_____ us wait an-y-more. We want our rights_____

Dm E A   Dm Am tacet- - - - Dm G   Dm

_____ and we don't care how.   We   want our Rev-o - lu - tion   Now!

8va bassa - ┘

Part 6

I first remember Dick Fariña at the festival in Indian Neck, Connecticut years ago, in a big summer house open for all the folkies on the eastern seaboard. It was a wet and windy weekend with lots of beer to enjoy and the music of a hundred banjos and guitar pickers. I think everybody was there that I had ever heard of, all the singers I loved to listen to. Eric Weissberg and the New Lost City Ramblers, Tom Rush and the old members of the Jim Queskin Jug-band, Logan English and the Beers family with their beautiful daughter and even Bob Shelton. Out under the trees in the rain I heard Reverend Gary Davis singing "Twelve Gates to the City." The weekend was just about perfect, full of nostalgia and friends I hadn't seen in a long while. Carolyn Hester was there, the darling of the folk scene, with her hair long and her sweet voice and her man. She was married to Dick then. When we went up to their room to get away from the noise of the banjos and guitars, I was nervous, frightened to sing for Richard. He was a handsome man, dark, with the eyes of a crazy Cuban and the slender face and body of a Spaniard, a Conquistador. It was years before I got over my initial awe of his nervous tension, his concealed vanity, his kindness in most things and his zeal for anything fun, anything gay, anything with action, farce or drama. We sat in the darkness of their room with a candle burning. Carolyn was in bed, the covers drawn up to her chin, her hair brushing her face and darkening her eyes. Richard sat across on the other bed, leaning toward her, and I sat on the end of her bed, my guitar in my hands and my heart in my throat. After I sang Dick smiled, and Carolyn smiled and yawned and we all talked a while in the candle-lit room and I felt better. Pretty soon I went off up to the bedroom I shared with Peter and Issy Gardner and a huge dog who snored all night. In the next room through paper thin walls, someone tried desperately and hopelessly to learn Scruggs picking on the banjo, and outside the rain dripped a sheath of sound over the big rambling house. It was quiet except for an occasional soft voice singing a ballad, and the hushed laughter and giggles of the banjo pickers huddled around the staircase drinking the last of the beer—and waiting for daylight when they could play the house awake.

Richard turned me on to a lot of things; his music and his writing and his love of yogurt with familia and peaches heaped on top. He loved to romp and hike along the Charles River with his big German Shepherd named Lush, who loved him so much he would have swum that big river for him and raced all the way to New York alongside the car; he would have done anything crazy and wild. All this because of the master with the dancing eyes and the loving, shouting, soothing voice. We were all a bit like that about Dick. The first time I went to visit him on Martha's Vineyard, when he was still married to Carolyn, he had become a "pretend" entrepreneur. He had arranged a little on-the-spot concert in the local church to make up expenses for the trip. I went over on the ferry from Wood's Hole, with my son, my husband and my oldest, dirtiest, raggedest clothes, and there Dick stood on the dock waiting for us, grinning his grin and surrounded with faces that reflected the same laughing, smiling mischievousness. Bruce Langhorne was there, and Carolyn, and Bruce's girl Ellen, and they all looked like cats that swallowed canaries. Beautiful Bruce Langhorne followed Dick with the same devotion and love that Lush did. But Bruce led, too, suggesting fiendish and impossible and silly trips and games that Richard jumped into like a Spaniel into a bird-pond. They had, they said, at Dick's suggestion, arranged a little surprise for us . . . and they took us through town in the car and pointed out all the posters that said concert tonight, with Carolyn Hester, Bruce Langhorne, David Gude and *featuring* Judy Collins.

Dick and Carolyn had a little house on the Chilmark pond, and Richard's first plan was to take us clamming with bare feet. We went in a canoe across the big pond, on the ocean side, and though there was only one other boat on the water, we promptly ran right smack into it. The man came out and started screaming at us and calling us a fine bunch of sailors . . . what were we doing on the boat if we couldn't sail and we just couldn't sail and we just couldn't stop from giggling. We caught an eel that Carolyn fried for dinner and in the middle of the night, what sounded like a bear or a burglar made a noise out in front of the house. It made a great rabbit stew the next day. It was so funny, those big guys, Fariña and Langhorne, tiptoeing heavily outside the door with the porch-light out, whispering huddled together, then spotting the noise and firing all at once at the poor luckless thing, then all bursting into laughter when they came back hauling their prey, his fuzzy tail still twitching in terror.

I read Dick's writing for the first time that summer on Martha's Vineyard. It was good, but it was going to get much better. I think at that time he must have just been starting his novel "Been Down So Long it Looks Like up to Me." There were a lot of poems and songs between that time and the release of the novel. There would be articles chronicling the life and times of the Baez family, and his attempts to sort himself out and put his own life into perspective.

I saw Dick again after he was married to Mimi Baez. I went to Monterey to sing in a festival at the fair grounds. Dick and Mimi showed up and stole me away to their house at the highlands on the way to Big Sur. They had a one-room wood house, big and warm and surrounded constantly with the dogs that wandered from miles away lured by Mimi's inability to let the smallest of them or the meanest go hungry. They lurked in a huge pack around the door, trading their avenged appetites for fierce protection of the house and Dick and Mimi. We fought our way through them and they stayed in a ring around the house, howling and barking protectively all night as we settled down in front of the fire with the shadows dancing and making patterns on our faces. We drank wine in blue enamelled silver cups, toasted their marriage and the Big Sur coast and I heard for the first time that lovely, fantasy-like music that they had just begun to make together, Mimi playing the guitar and Richard the dulcimer and their two voices intertwining and running in and out of the string sounds. Eventually Newport Folk Festival would hear it and go wild for it, the gentleness of it enriching Dick's rock and roll songs with something rare and beautiful.

When the Fariñas moved to Cambridge I saw them a lot more. I would stay with them sometimes and sometimes they would come down to New York and stay with me. When I lost custody of Clark, Dick would have done anything, if he had been able to think of a scheme that would work to help me get Clark back. He would rant and rave about courts and injustice. He felt my separation and understood what it did to me. He was kind about it, funny, sometimes making me laugh when it was too, too painful to cry.

I've always thought that Richard was just breaking through into some greater perception of himself and other people when he died. He knew there was someone at home inside his wildly imaginative head, and he was starting to come into contact with it, to let it out. When we had parties he helped to make them into mad happenings. But late at night when everyone had given up and gone home after a party in Cambridge or here in New York, after Dick had made an incredible dinner and everyone had eaten themselves sick and gone to sleep, we talked about things we felt deeply. I think we would have gotten to know each other and like each other even more if he had lived. His music was becoming more and more important to him and also to me. On my fifth album, he played the dulcimer and Mimi and Bruce and the dog and a bunch of other characters and I had the best time I think I ever had recording. It's so silly to be adults sometimes. We were all kids who should have been left in the playground most of the time. The ones who love to put pie in the face and hands in the mouth and play grownup, ah, silly, silly. Lush lept about in the middle of the studio, slamming into the microphones and entangling himself in the wires and Dick played the dulcimer and wrestled with Lush and we ended up making a beautiful album in the madness and fun.

Richard's funeral had a life of its own. May, 1966, three years ago . . . Carmel Valley . . . Richard's parents, his mother sitting on a foam rubber donut because she was having trouble with her back. Someone had to carry the donut around behind her, she had to put it on the chair beside the coffin before she could sit down—Richie would have laughed—to weep over her boy's body. The rain, the clouds hanging over the beach where Mimi and her older sister Pauline and I went in our black veiled dresses to run the dog on the beach, the big honey-colored animal who couldn't understand why the girls took him to run in the morning fog and cloud, on a strange beach far from the Big Sur highlands. Cutting bangs on Pauline's long hair the night before the funeral, sleeping-no-sleep in a big bunch, finding no sleep, no reason for the premonitions that Mimi had had and others. Dreams, messages, thoughts, messages. Why did he give me his keys, she said, when he left drunken, happy, late-night-reveler at his own party, the party for the release of his book. Why did he give her his keys when she doesn't drive, never has driven. Why in the rain, on a motorcycle, why so fast, with a stranger, with the fulfilled promise lying like a bunch of flowers in his hands, printed and posted and parcelled—one of the best books I ever read, before his death, thank God. No music for two days, could not bear, could not have borne to hear one slipping-slinging, yanking-your-pain-from-you note. Before his book was finished, about near the last chapter, his hand became paralyzed, couldn't move, it couldn't write a word, not until he realized he didn't want to, didn't want to finish it because maybe he couldn't accept Dick Fariña succeeding, being whole, being on his own two feet having succeeded at something only he could have done in the first place. Why rain-dark strange riding running from the scene of the successful crime. I did not look into the coffin.

They are going to make Richard's book into a movie now, a wonderful, wide-lens technicolor marvel that should star one of Dick's still surviving and kicking old friends, like Bruce Langhorne or Alfredo, wild-eyed like Dick was, full of the old piss and vinegar and ready, to go or not to go, axing his way to a living in Alaska. Lush lives there now, in the woods with Alfredo, romping with another dark, beautiful-haired, fiery-eyed wild crazy man.

The dog was nervous and ran around and around the graveyard, and everyone began to smile, because Dick would have laughed out loud even while the little bunches of flowers were being dropped on him. We stood around a while and then left for what should have been the wake. Inside the house, they were playing music; Ray Charles, the kind of music Richard liked.

This is part of the poem he wrote for me, for my fifth album, a year before I stood in front of his grave:

> *"The time for telling then,*
> *no matter what the nature*
> *of the private tale,*
> *could still be chosen*
> *at another's whim.*
> *The siren, train, and horn,*
> *the fortune whimpering upon your palm,*
> *the quick, unspoken cry*
> *of chaos in the molecules of welded air*
> *could still have counterparts*
> *on yet another understanding tongue.*
> *And hearing what you feel*
> *is known can make you pause*
> *(while standing at whatever tomb)*
> *and give a second silent thought*
> *to going back the way you came."*

When Joni writes she finds the words
that unthread the confusion and paint scenes as vivid
and distinct as her water colors. When she sings the circle is completed.

michael from mountains

Words and Music by Joni Mitchell

With motion, lyrically

Mi - chael wakes you up with sweets, He takes you up streets, and the rain comes down,

Optional with 2nd and 3rd verse

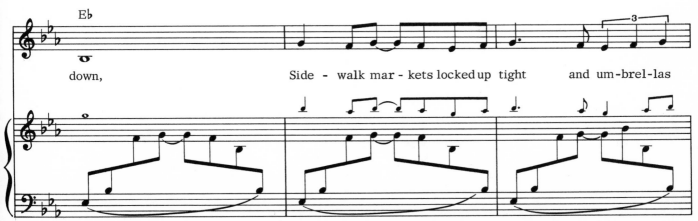

Side - walk mar - kets locked up tight and um-brel-las

will go to, Know____ that I_____ will know you.

Some-day I may know you ver - y well._____

Last time only

i.h.

2. Michael brings you to a park,
   He sings, and it's dark when the clouds come by.
   Yellow slickers up on swings,
   Like puppets on strings hanging in the sky.
   They'll splash home to suppers in wall-papered kitchens
   Their Mothers will scold,
   But Michael will hold you to keep away cold
   Till the sidewalks are dry.

   Chorus:
   Michael from mountains,
   Go where you will go to,
   Know that I will know you.
   Someday I may know you very well.

3. Michael leads you up the stairs,
   He needs you to care and you know you do.
   Cats come crying to the key
   And dry you will be in a towel or two.
   There's rain in the window and sun in the painting
   That smiles on the wall,
   You want to know all, but his mountains have called
   So you never do.
   Chorus

since you've asked

Words and Music by Judy Collins

What I'll give you since you asked is all my time to-geth-er;

Take the rug-ged, sun-ny days, the warm and Rock-y weath-er,

Take the roads that I have walked a-long, look-ing for to-mor-row's

194

Sisters of Mercy

With movement, and delicately

Words and Music by Leonard Cohen

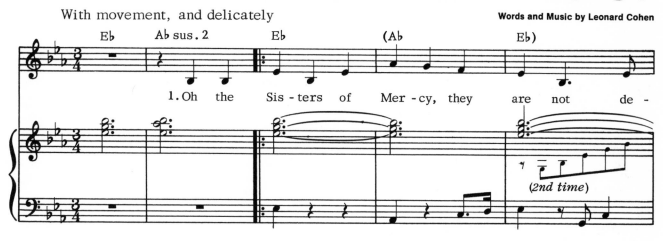

1. Oh the Sis-ters of Mer-cy, they are not de-

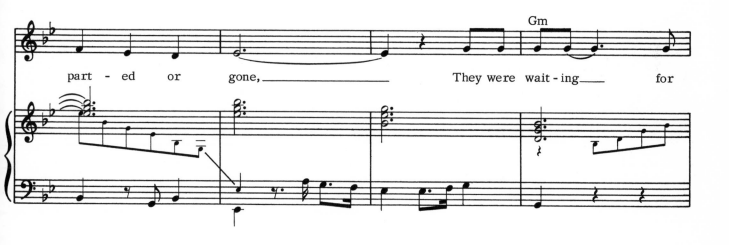

part-ed or gone, They were wait-ing for

me when I thought that I just can't go on.

trol._____ It be-gins with your fam-'ly and soon it___ comes

'round to your soul._____ I've been where you're hang-ing, I think I can

see how you're pinned;_____ When you're not feel-ing ho-ly, your

lone-li-ness says that you've sinned. 3. They

right.   We were lov - ers like that,   and be - sides,   it would

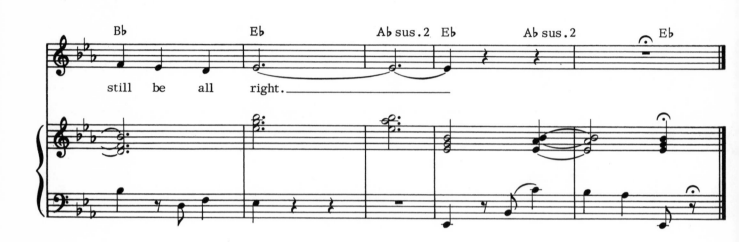

still   be   all   right._____

3. They lay down beside me,
   I made my confession to them.
   They touched both my eyes
   And I touched the dew on their hem.
   If your life is a leaf
   That the seasons tear off and condemn,
   They will bind you with love
   That is graceful and green as a stem.

4. When I left they were sleeping.
   I hope you run into them soon.
   Don't turn on the lights,
   You can read their address by the moon,
   And it won't make me jealous
   If I learned that they sweetened your night.
   We weren't lovers like that
   And besides it would still be all right . . .
   We weren't lovers like that
   And besides it would still be all right.

priests

Like a chant, sung freely but with a steady accompaniment

Words and Music by Leonard Cohen

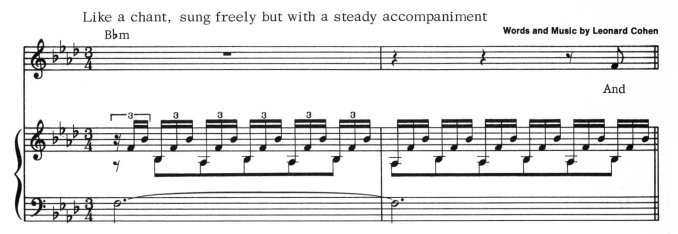

And

who_____ will write love

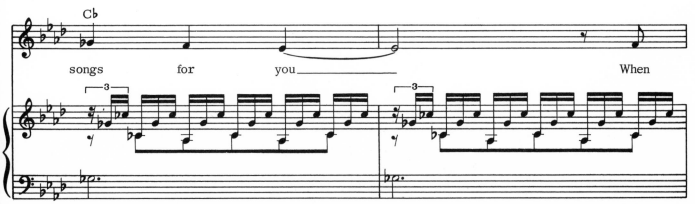

songs   for   you_____   When

turned to lace,

all your ar-mor has

turned _____ to lace.

2. My priests they will put flowers there,
   They kneel before the glass,
   But they'll wear away your little window, love,
   They will trample on the grass,
   They will trample on the grass.

3. And who will shoot the arrow
   That men will follow through your grace.
   And when I'm Lord of memories
   And all your armor has turned to lace,
   And all your armor has turned to lace.

4. The simple life of heroes,
   The twisted life of saints,
   May just confuse the sunny calendar
   With their red and golden paint,
   With their red and golden paint.

5. And all of you have seen the dance
   That God has kept from me,
   But he has seen me watching you
   When all your minds were free,
   When all your minds were free.

6. And who will write love songs for you
   When I am low'red at last
   And your body is the little highway shrine
   That all my priests have passed,
   That all my priests have passed.

7. My priests they will put flowers there,
   They will stand before the glass,
   But they'll wear away your little window, love,
   They will trample on the grass,
   They will trample on the grass.

Whether she sings in her stained-glass and dark wood house
in Laurel Canyon or on the stage in multicolored lights, Joni takes you on trips
interwoven with magic and the secret of what it feels like to be a woman.

BOTH SIDES NOW

Words and Music by Joni Mitchell

Moderately, flowing

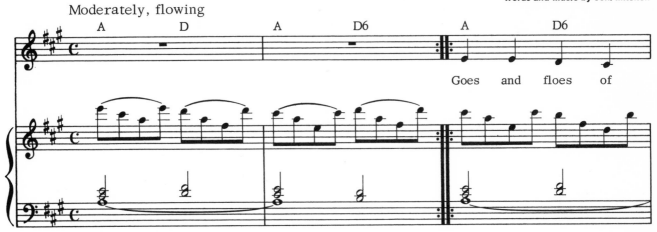

Goes and floes of

an - gel hair___ and ice - cream cas - tles___ in the air and

feath - ered can - yons___ ev-'ry-where;   I've looked at clouds

2. Moons and Junes and ferris wheels,
   The dizzy, dancing way you feel;
   When ev'ry fairy tale comes real,
   I've looked at love that way.
   But now it's just another show
   You leave 'em laughing when you go;
   And if you care, don't let them know,
   Don't give yourself away.

   Chorus:
   I've looked at love from both sides now,
   From win and lose, and still somehow,
   It's love's illusions I recall,
   I really don't know love at all.

3. Tears and fears and feeling proud,
   To say I love you right out loud;
   Dreams and schemes and circus crowds,
   I've looked at life that way.
   But now old friends are acting strange,
   They shake their heads, they say I've changed;
   Well, something's lost and something's gained
   In living every day.

   Chorus:
   I've looked at life from both sides now,
   From win and lose, and still somehow,
   It's life's illusions I recall,
   I really don't know life at all.

HEY, THAT'S NO WAY TO SAY GOODBYE

Words and Music by Leonard Cohen

I loved you in the morn - - ing, our kiss-es deep and

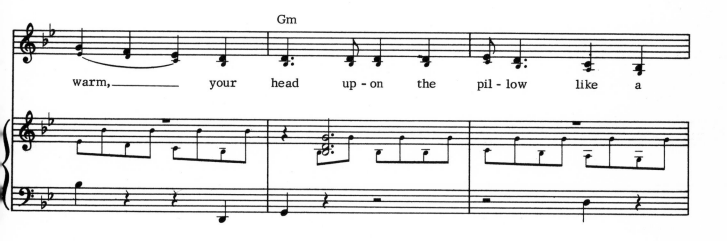

warm, _____ your head up-on the pil - low like a

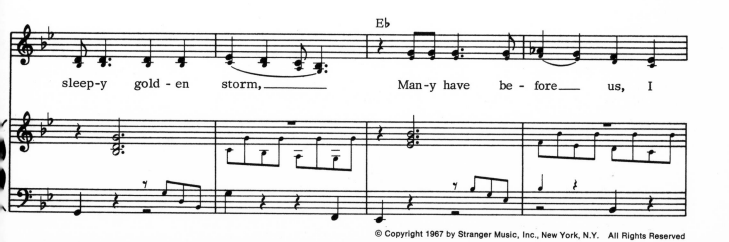

sleep-y gold - en storm, _____ Man-y have be-fore ___ us, I

that's   no   way___   to   say___   Good - bye._____

Fine

I'm not   look-ing   for   an - oth-er   as   I   wan - der   in   my   time_____

Walk   me   to   the   cor   -   ner,   our   steps   will   al - ways   rhyme._____

You   know   my   love   goes   with   you   as   your   love   stays   with   me_____

It's just the way it chang-es like the shore-line and the sea;

Let's not talk of love or change or things we can't un - tie.

Your eyes are soft with sor - row___ Hey, that's___ no

way___ to say___ good - bye.___

D.C. al Fine

This song began as I stood looking out on the Atlantic Ocean near Newport, R.I. in a sleepless sunrise. It went on to New York, growing restless to be done. In Colorado, near Aspen, it began to hatch, and I finally finished it in David and Sheryl's backyard in the hills of Los Angeles.

albatross

Words and music by Judy Collins

Come a - way a - lone.

2. Even now by the gate
   With your long hair blowing,
   And the colors of the day
   That lie along your arms,
   You must barter your life
   To make sure you are living,
   And the crowd that has come,
   You give them the colors,
   And the bells and wind and the dreams.
   Will there never be a prince
   Who rides along the sea and the mountains,
   Scattering the sand and foam
   Into amethyst fountains,
   Riding up the hills from the beach
   In the long summer grass,
   Holding the sun in his hands
   And shattering the isinglass?
   Day and night and day again,
   And people come and go away forever,
   While the shining summer sea
   Dances in the glass of your mirror,
   While you search the waves for love
   And your visions for a sign,
   The knot of tears around your throat
   Is crystalizing into your design . . .

Chorus:
And in the night the iron wheels
   rolling through the rain
Down the hills through the long grass
   to the sea,
And in the dark the hard bells
   ringing with pain,
Come away alone . . .
Come away alone . . . with me.

La Chanson Des Vieux Amants

Words by Jacques Brel   Music by Jacques Brel and Gerard Jouannest

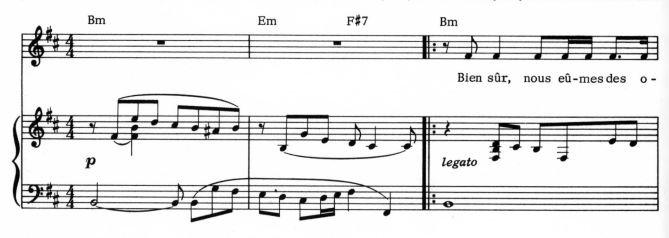

Bien sûr, nous eû-mes des o-

ra - ges   Vingt ans d'a-mour c'est l'a-mour fol

Mil-le fois tu pris ton ba-ga - ge   Mil-le fois je pris mon en-

221

2. Moi, je sais tous tes sortilèges
   Tu sais tous mes envoûtements
   Tu m'as gardé de pièges en pièges
   Je t'ai perdue de temps en temps
   Bien sûr tu pris quelques amants
   Il fallait bien passer le temps
   Il faut bien que le corps exulte
   Finalement, finalement
   Il nous fallu bien du talent
   Pour être vieux sans être adultes
   Refrain

3. Et plus le temps nous fait cortège
   Et plus le temps nous fait tourment
   Mais n'est ce pas le pire piège
   Que vivre en paix pour des amants
   Bien sûr tu pleures un peu moins tôt
   Je me déchire un peu plus tard
   Nous protégeons moins nos mystères
   On laisse moins faire le hasard
   On se méfie du fil de l'eau
   Mais c'est toujours la tendre guerre.
   Refrain

Part 7

It is Sunday, and I am on my way back from visiting my son at camp. I drive into town in a taxi, dressed in old dungarees and a red rainproof slicker, my hair done up in a wind-blown knot. My sister Holly is with me, her hair sunbleached and blowing in the hot breeze from the city, her brown eyes staring out across the Triboro Bridge as we ride in from La Guardia Airport. In my lap is a cardboard box filled with potted plants from the greenhouse of my friends, the Baumans, who run an arts camp in the Berkshires. Clark is at camp near there and yesterday I saw him; his hair is blonding red and his face fuller than ever with freckles. He has grown, tall for his ten and a half years; he showed me a salamander he caught. It was translucent orange-peach colored, with little green spots on it. You could almost see through it. We picked blueberries and avoided the poison ivy and the snakes that Clark promises are in the big rock next to the blueberry patch. The countryside is beautiful, Clark is happy and this morning as Holly and I are leaving to come back to the city the rain threads its way in curtains through the gigantic trees that bend and roll with the New England countryside. My mind is full of the smells and quiet of the country, and the return to my city of millions will be a shock. But as I fly through the clouds in the single-engine executive airplane from Pittsfield, I realize that I am glad to be coming home. The city is full of dirt and noise and constant frustration; the traffic is terrible, the rents are high and it is a brutal place for a child or an adult to grow up. But my greatest joys, my severest pain, most of my closest friends are here. It is my home, and Clark's home. Four years ago I moved up from the little village apartment on Hudson Street to the upper west side. I got a big, rambling apartment. I share the neighborhood with whores, junkies, down-and-out winos, airline stewardesses, antique-store owners, bookies, dentists, actors, psychologists and psychiatrists, and a lady who trains young mothers in the old art of having babies naturally, without drugs. She lives in my building, and when there are six or seven pregnant ladies in the elevator with their respective husbands, the elevator groans and creaks and rides low to the fifth floor where it lands inches below the floor level. They clamber out, awkward in their maternity clothes, carrying the new lives in their full beautiful bellies.

In the middle of this island city, where there is filth and the little children wade in the firehouse fountains between the avenues, there is one of the most beautiful parks in the world. It stretches green and big through the very middle of the city. There are lakes and fountains and theaters and thousands of trees in it. I spent two months in Central Park this summer, doing Henrik Ibsen's "Peer Gynt." It was one of the most peaceful and contented times of my life. I got to know some beautiful people and learned a little about the theater, about that wonderful and magic thing that happens when you are interacting with others on the stage. Every day I ate Italian ices and 30¢ hot dogs in the shade of the trees along the lake in back of the Delacourt Theater. When it was hot we stretched out our legs and faces in the sun. There were other pale Irish like me; we put zinc oxide on our noses and took salt pills and wore hats to keep the sun off when it got too hot at noon. When I wasn't watching rehearsals I found quiet shady places and watched the moving pattern of color: the kids biking, the old people sitting on benches, girls walking sometimes five great hairy, silky dogs with weird foreign names. There is a big castle behind the theater, on the other side of the lake, and the reflection of the wooden stage-set lay in stark patterns across its walls at night. During the play, when I wasn't on stage, I would sit on the stones, looking out across the dark lake. I played Solveig, the girl who waits for Peer Gynt, while he searches and roams the world, looking for himself in all the unlikely and peculiar places men look. In the end he finds himself in Solveig who loves him, and had loved him all along.

In the last five nights of performance, we made a movie. After the performances at night we would have supper by the lake at midnight, and film until the sun came up over the buildings of Fifth Avenue. In those nights, in the middle of the deserted park, in the middle of the biggest city in the country, we were like a band of refugees huddling under the stage when the rain drove us in, napping on cots with our costumes thrown over us, watching the still lake and the big quiet sky over Manhattan's towering skyscrapers. We finished the movie under the bleachers of Delacourt Theater at eight o'clock on a Monday morning. As I left the theatre with Stacy Keach, my Peer Gynt, New York awoke around us, all slickers and galoshes, trying to keep dry. We walked from the world of Henrik Ibsen into our city, hurrying together under one umbrella through the green park.

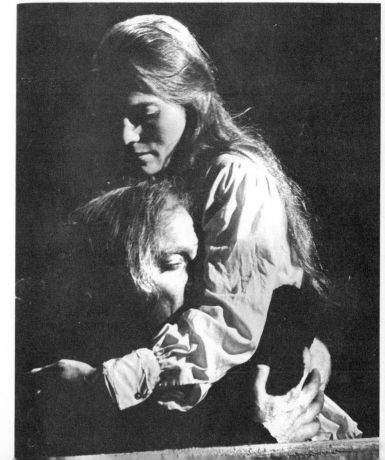

Who Knows Where The Time Goes

Words and Music by Sandy Denny

A - cross the morn-ing sky   All the birds are   leav - - - -

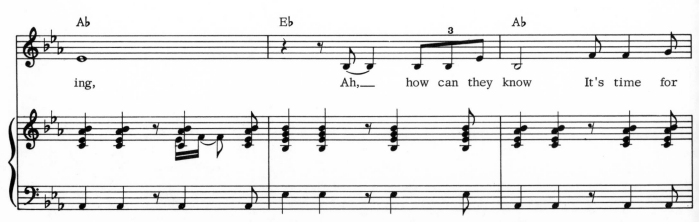

ing,   Ah,___ how can they know   It's time for

2. Sad deserted shore
   Your fickle friends are leaving,
   Ah, but then you know
   It's time for them to go,
   But I will still be here,
   I have no thought of leaving,
   I do not count the time,
   Who knows where the time goes?
   Who knows where the time goes?

3. And I'm not going
   While my love is near me,
   And I know it will be so,
   Till it's time to go,
   So come the storms of winter
   And the birds of spring again,
   I do not fear the time,
   Who knows how my love grows?
   Who knows where the time goes?

I've known this song of Ian's for years,
and one night in California Steve Stills and I were singing it in the car
on the way in from Topanga Canyon. I said: "That's beautiful."
He said: "Why don't you record it." So we did.

some Day soon

Words and Music by Ian Tyson

1. There's a young man that I know, His age is twen-ty - one,
par - ents can - not stand him, 'Cause he rides the ro - de - o,

Comes from down in south-ern Col - o - rad - o,
My fa - ther says that he will leave me cry - in',

So blow, you old blue north - ern,__ Blow my love to me, He's driv - in' in to -night__ from Cal - i - for - nia, He loves his damned ol' ro - de - o__ As much as he loves me, Some-day soon,_____ go - in' with__ him, some-day soon.

Some-day soon,__ go-in' with him, some-day soon.__

THE STORY OF ISAAC

Words and Music by Leonard Cohen

1. The door it o-pened slow-ly and my fa-ther he came in,
2. You who build these al-tars now to sac-ri-fice these chil-dren,

I was nine years old.
You must not do it an-y-more.

And he stood so tall a -
For you nev - er had a

bove me, / vi - sion,

and his blue eyes they were shin - ing / and you nev - er have been tempt-ed

And his voice was ver - y / By the dev - il of the

cold. / Lord.

He said, "I've had a vi - sion, / Yes, you who stand a - bove them now,

and you know I'm strong and ho - ly, / your hatch-ets blunt and blood - y,

I must do what I've been told. / You were not there be - fore.

So he start-ed up the moun-tain, / When I lay up-on the moun-tain,

I was run-ning, he was / and my fa-ther's hand was

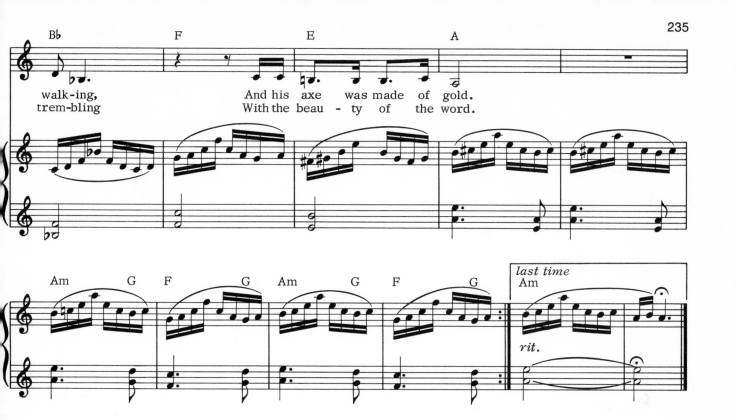

walk-ing,
trem-bling

And his axe was made of gold.
With the beau - ty of the word.

3. And if you call me brother now
   Forgive me if I ask
   "According to whose plan?"
   And when all has come to dust,
   I will kill you if I must,
   I will love you if I can,
   And may I never learn to scorn,
   The body out of chaos born;
   The woman and the man.
   Have mercy on our uniform
   Man of peace, man of war
   The peacock spreads his fan.

BIRD ON THE WIRE

Words and Music by Leonard Cohen

Gospel style

I hope you know_____ that it was not to you._____ 2. Like a

D.S. al Fine

2. Like a baby, stillborn,
   Like a beast with his horn,
   I have torn everyone who reached out to me.
   But I swear by this song
   And by all that I have done wrong
   That I will, I will make it all, all up to thee.

   I saw a man, a beggar leaning on his crutch,
   He said to me, "Why do you ask for so much?"
   There was a woman, a woman leaning in a door,
   She said, "Why not, why not, why not, why not
   ask for more?"

   Like a bird on the wire
   Like a drunk in a midnight choir
   I have tried in my way, to be free.

First Boy I Loved

Words and Music by Robin Williamson

2. We parted so hard
   Me rushing round Britain with a guitar
   Making love to people
   That I didn't even like to see.
   Well, I would think of you
   Yes, I mean in the sick, sad morning
   And in the lonely mid-night
   Try to hold your face before me.

   Chorus:
   And I want you to know, I just had to go,
   And I want you to know, we just had to grow.
   And your probably married now, kids and all,
   And you turned into a grown-up male stranger,
   And if I was lying with you now
   I wouldn't be here at all.

3. I never slept with you
   Though we must have made love a thousand times,
   For we were just young—didn't have no place to go.
   Yet in the wide hills by many the long water
   You have gathered flowers—and did they not smell for me.

   Chorus:
   And I want you to know, we just had to grow,
   And I want you to know, I just had to go.
   So it's goodbye first love and I hope your fine;
   I am a sweet man's woman
   Maybe some day to have babies fine,
   He's a true friend of mine.

I PITY THE POOR IMMIGRANT

Words and Music by Bob Dylan

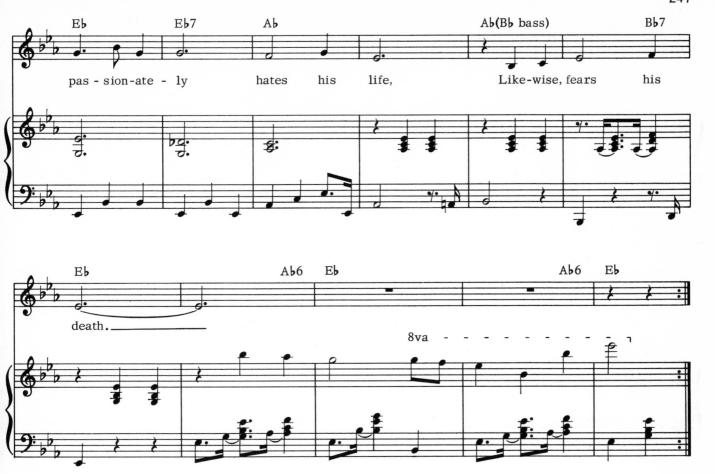

2. I pity the poor immigrant
   Whose strength is all in vain,
   Whose heaven is like iron sides,
   Whose tears fall like rain,
   Who eats but is not satisfied,
   Who hears but does not see,
   Who falls in love with wealth itself,
   And turns his back on me.

3. I pity the poor immigrant
   Who tramples through the mud,
   Who fills his mouth with laughing,
   And who fills his tongue with blood,
   Whose visions in their final end
   Must shatter like the glass,
   I pity the poor immigrant
   When his gladness comes to pass.

my FatHer

Lyrically, nostalgic

Words and Music by Judy Collins

fa - ther al - ways prom - ised us____ that we____ would live____ in

France, We'd go boat - ing on the Seine___ and I would learn to

2. All my sisters soon were gone
    to Denver and Cheyenne,
Marrying their grownup dreams,
    the lilacs and the man.
I stayed behind the youngest still,
    only danced alone,
The colors of my father's dreams
    faded without a sigh.

3. And I live in Paris now,
    my children dance and dream
Hearing the ways of a miner's life
    in words they've never seen.
I sail my memories afar
    like boats across the Seine,
And watch the Paris sun
    set in my father's eyes again.

4. *Repeat 1st Verse*

PHOTO NOTES

Front End Paper: At the Forest Hills Music Festival, 1967.
(Photo by Peter Raymond-Polymenakos)

Page 2: Recording the JUDY COLLINS' FIFTH ALBUM, 1965.
(Photo by Suzanne Szasz)

Pages 14-15: *(top left)* Baby Judy.
(2nd row, left to right) First birthday candle. With Grandfather Booth. Christmas with David and Michael.
(bottom row, left to right) Judy keeping cool in backyard. Judy, age 11. Judy, age 2, and friendly cows. Father, Judy, and Michael. David, Michael, Judy, Denver-John, father, mother. Father as a boy.
(Photos from the Collins family album)

Page 36: With Mimi Fariña and Lush, 1965.
(Photo by Suzanne Szasz)

Page 40: Judy and Clark at home, New York City, 1965.
(Photo by Suzanne Szasz)

Page 64: Judy, 1964.
(Photo by Suzanne Szasz)

Page 65: *(top)* Backstage at Carnegie Hall with Steven Stills, 1968.
(Photo by Julie Snow)
(bottom) Judy and Eric Weissberg, with Mimi and Dick Fariña in background, 1965.
(Photo by Suzanne Szasz)

Page 94: With Leonard Cohen at the Newport Folk Festival, 1967.
(Photo found in Judy's guitar case, August 1969)

Page 118: *(top)* Judy at home, New York City, 1967.
(Photo by Jackie Paull)
(bottom left) With sister Holly-Ann, 1968.
(Photo by Julie Snow)
(bottom right) Judy and Michael Thomas at St. Johns University, 1969.
(Photo by Julie Snow)

Page 136: *(top)* On tour, spring 1969.
(Photo by Julie Snow)
(bottom) Carnegie Hall posters.
(Photo by Julie Snow)

Page 181: Dick and Mimi Fariña, March 1966.
(Photo by Julie Snow)

Page 182: *(top, left to right)* Harold Leventhal, Dick and Mimi Fariña, Mark Abramson, Judy, and Lush, at recording session, 1965.
(Photo by Suzanne Szasz)
(bottom) Dick Fariña and Judy, New York City, 1965.
(Photo by Suzanne Szasz)

Page 225: *(top)* With Stacy Keach in Central Park, during rehearsal break, summer 1969.
(Photo by Julie Snow)
(bottom) Judy and Stacy during the filming of "Peer Gynt", Central Park, 1969.
(Photo by Julie Snow)

Page 251: Judy, 1967.
(Photo by Julie Snow)

Back End Paper: Clark at Forest Hills Music Festival, 1968.
(Photo by Julie Snow)

Cover: Courtesy of Electra Records.
(Photo by Jim Frawley)

A JUDY COLLINS DISCOGRAPHY

WHO KNOWS WHERE THE TIME GOES • EKS-74033

Hello, Hooray
Story of Isaac
My Father
Someday Soon
Who Knows Where the Time Goes
Pity the Poor Immigrant
First Boy I Loved
Bird on the Wire
Pretty Polly

WILDFLOWERS • EKS-74012

Michael From Mountains
Since You Asked
Sisters of Mercy
Priests
A Ballata of Francesco Landini: Lasso! di donna
Both Sides Now
La Chanson des vieux amants
Sky Fell
Albatross
Hey, That's No Way to Say Goodbye

IN MY LIFE • EKS-7320

Just Like Tom Thumb's Blues
Hard Lovin' Loser
Pirate Jenny
Suzanne
La Colombe
Marat/Sade
I Think It's Going to Rain Today
Sunny Goodge Street
Liverpool Lullaby
Dress Rehearsal Rag
In My Life

JUDY COLLINS FIFTH ALBUM • EKS-7300

Pack Up Your Sorrows
The Coming Of The Roads
So Early, Early In The Spring
Tomorrow Is A Long Time
Daddy You've Been On My Mind
Thirsty Boots
Mr. Tambourine Man
Lord Gregory
In The Heat Of The Summer
Early Morning Rain
Carry It On
It Isn't Nice

THE JUDY COLLINS CONCERT • EKS-7280

Winter Sky
The Last Thing On My Mind

Tear Down the Walls
Bonnie Boy is Young
Me and My Uncle
Wild Rippling Water
The Lonesome Death of Hattie Carroll
Ramblin' Boy
Red-Winged Blackbird
Coal Tattoo
Cruel Mother
Bottle of Wine
Medgar Evers Lullaby
Hey, Nelly, Nelly

JUDY COLLINS #3 • EKS-7243

Anathea
Bullgure Run
Farewell
Hey, Nelly, Nelly
Ten O'Clock All Is Well
The Dove
Masters of War
In the Hills of Shiloh
The Bells of Rhymney
Deportee
Settle Down
Come Away Melinda
Turn! Turn! Turn!

GOLDEN APPLES OF THE SUN • EKS-7222

Golden Apples of the Sun
Bonnie Ship the Diamond
Little Brown Dog
Twelve Gates to the City
Christ Child Lullaby
Great Selchie of Shule Skerry
Tell Me Who I'll Marry
Fannerio
Crow on the Cradle
Lark in the Morning
Sing Hallelujah
Shule Aroon

A MAID OF CONSTANT SORROW • EKS-7209

Maid of Constant Sorrow
The Prickilie Bush
Wild Mountain Thyme
Tim Evans
Sailor's Life
Wars of Germany
O Daddy Be Gay
I know Where I'm Going
John Riley
Pretty Saro
The Rising of the Moon

exclusively on ELEKTRA RECORDS